KANGAROO'S COMMENTS
&
WALLABY'S WORDS

KANGAROO'S COMMENTS & WALLABY'S WORDS

The Aussie Word Book

Helen Jonsen

Illustrations by
John Colquhoun

HIPPOCRENE BOOKS
New York

For information, address:
Hippocrene Books, Inc.
171 Madison Ave.
New York, NY 10016

Library of Congress Cataloging-in-Publication Data

Jonsen, Helen.
    Kangaroo's comments and Wallaby's words : the Aussie word book /
    Helen Jonsen ; illustrations by John Colquhoun.
        168 p. 31½×48cm.
        Bibliography: p. 167
        Includes index.
        ISBN 0-87052-580-8 (pbk.)
        1. English language—Provincialisms—Australia—Dictionaries. 2. English language—Provincialisms—Australia. 3. Australia—Civilization. I. Title.
    PE3601.Z5J64   1988
    427'.994—dc19   88-21652
                                                          CIP

Printed in the United States of America

To My Wallaby

Contents

Acknowledgments

Each of us has seen plenty of television award shows where winners stand at the podium and thank everyone from kindergarten teachers to dogs. Producers do not give enough time to publicly thank co-workers and teachers, friends and loved ones. Film makers indulge in credits at the end of their movies, noting everyone from the stars and director right down the list to the "best boy" and "assistant grip."

Writers and publishers stop short at those kinds of credits. You will not find a page that lists the typesetters and publicity people; but the author gets a chance to indulge in this section called Acknowledgments. There are innumerable people who made possible *Kangaroo's Comments and Wallaby's Words*, too many to mention by name, only by association. I hope no one feels left out.

Australia has been an interest of mine since I wrote an eighth-grade paper on the world's animals. Marsupials topped my list of interests, especially "God's little joke," the platypus. It was many years before I was introduced intimately to the wondrous world Down Under by Mark Watkins, the Australian who later married me. It was Mark who asked, **"Can I bot a chewie?"**

and sent me in search of other words and phrases used by Australians, but not Americans. He has contributed to the list for several years now and put up with me through lulls and deadlines.

His family, now my family, with their zest for life, has introduced me especially to the Sunshine State of Queensland.

But, I suppose every writer must thank the person who first offered the opportunity to read, write and enjoy everything. That's where my mother comes in. She was not a novelist or journalist. She did not keep a diary and yet she chronicled her life and our lives, through letters and notes to friends and family around the world. She brought joy through her lovely flowing script and loving correspondence. It was her legacy. Her neatness, her grammar, her painstaking choice of words were handed down to me unwittingly. She studied with me; she proofread my papers and sent them back for rewrites. Catherine Browne Johnson was my first editor, a staunch one, a loving one.

I thank my sister, Mary Giovannucci too, for always reminding me there is a big world out there and I should go out and discover it. And to my father, Fred C. Johnson, brothers and their families, and my closest friends, Betty Lidke and Mary Marino, for putting up with a journalist's transient and changeable lifestyle—for accepting all the times I couldn't be there and still being happy when I could be—I am grateful.

As for this study of Australian-English, every Australian I have ever met contributed to this book. In the early stages, there were Arthur Higgins and Phil Hanna baffling me with their rhyming slang on the docks of Newport, R.I.; and later there was the encouragement from my compatriots at Network Ten in Melbourne.

Acknowledgments

During the final stages in New York, the Wisemans and O'Ferralls contributed ideas that blossomed into pages.

Aside from the Aussies, there are those who believed from the beginning, like Linda Bezold who encouraged me to keep going from ten thousand miles away, and John Colquhoun, who offered his creative talents long before we had a publisher.

A few other people must be noted, too: Dennis D'Agostino, for proving it could be done by 30; Joseph Frese, S.J., a talented writer and teacher who pushed me one more time at the right time; Tom Barritt, for showing a writer's stick-to-it-ness; Jon Foley, for giving me an inspired gift on my way to Australia—*The Writer's Art* by James Kilpatrick; and Mr. Kilpatrick for inspiring a writer he never met; Clare Kain for taking on the typing and being a close and dear friend when I most needed one. Finally, thanks to George Blagowidow of Hippocrene Books for believing in a first-time author.

Kangaroo's Comments and Wallaby's Words: The Aussie Word Book is a culmination of all these unflinching spirits and encouragements. It would be nothing without each of them and all of them behind me.

"Taa!"
Helen Jonsen

Preface

"Can I bot a chewie?" Regardless of what accent this question is asked with, it stands out as an odd phrase and the meaning is unknown to most Americans. Yet, the phrase is common English—easily understood in The Land Down Under.

In Australian-English **"Can I bot a chewie?"** means "May I borrow a piece of gum?"

With that in mind it becomes obvious Australians speak a different brand of English than Americans do. This book endeavors to explain the labels, words and phrases (not the accents) which might befuddle an unknowing Yank first confronted by the Aussie tongue. It is meant to be a light-hearted look at the English language broadened and colored by the customs, climate and colloquialisms adopted Down Under that are distinct from those used in the U.S.A.

For those familiar with British-English, some of the phrases will not sound strange because Aussies employ many British phrases in their day-to-day speech. The most common ones are noted in these pages.

This is not meant to be a definitive lexicon of Australian-English. It would take a tome divided into several volumes to complete such a task, and in the end, it

13

would be a book touched only by scholars and researchers and stored on library shelves.

Instead, I hope this is a "readable" book of everyday speech, which can be picked up at leisure and shared among friends—whether they are travelers or just people interested in learning more about the English language.

It seems appropriate for *Kangaroo's Comments and Wallaby's Words* to be published in 1988, the 200th anniversary of the founding of Australia as a British penal colony. The bicentennial has been planned as a year-long party, a year when Australia is reaching out to the world, saying, "Hey, look me over!" Australians started New Year 1988 with an extravagant live television tour of their nation beamed by satellite around the world. Brisbane is the host city for the 1988 World Expo and many other events are planned for overseas visitors to share the heritage and rich natural wonders of the vast Land Down Under.

Australians have become a proud people, no longer the stepchildren of Mother England. Their country is a melting pot, like the United States, and their language and young culture reflect that.

Kangaroo's Comments and Wallaby's Words is concerned mainly with the language of Oz. Many factors shape the spoken tongue of a country and that later shapes the literature as well. Australia's isolation, before mass media, had a heavy impact and so did its early beginnings as a prison colony, home to lower classes of British society complete with the jargon and slang of the streets. Native aborigines salted the tongue with their words and phrases to describe things no white man had ever seen before.

As the Australians take this year to look behind and plan ahead, let's join them in celebrating their

Preface

uniqueness in the English-speaking world. Every Australian I've met or spoken to over the years, and every book or article, poem or lyrics, I've had a chance to read has contributed to this collection. I hope you enjoy reading it as much as I've enjoyed compiling it.

"Cheers!"
Helen Jonsen
Melbourne 1985/New York 1988

How to Use This Book

Kangaroo's Comments and Wallaby's Words is not a scholarly book, although factual, but is meant to be read and enjoyed at an easy pace, like life in Australia. To make it even more enjoyable, all the Australian words and phrases used in the eight chapters have been printed in bold print in their first reference. In addition, the terms are listed alphabetically in the Australian-American glossary in the back of the book. There you will find quick American definitions, as well as the chapters in which the words are discussed. So you can check on Aussie words you might have heard elsewhere even though you haven't yet found them in the book.

Part One

Part One

CHAPTER ONE

Speaking of Australia

What are submarine sandwiches called where you live? Hoagies? Grinders? Subs? Heroes? Or wedges? All of these different words from different regions of America describe the same thing: two pieces of bread with food in between. Now, have you heard of a **sanger** or a **jaffle?** They're sandwich names in the English language too, but not American-English.

They appear in a legitimate dictionary containing words spoken in a country located in the opposite hemisphere from England and America, more than ten thousand miles away. There, English has been created anew by a colorful people who developed new words to describe unusual animals, birds and plants, and home-grown household and farm articles and doings. The isolation of the people became a fertile field for seedlings of an old tongue to blossom into a cross-pollinated hybrid.

The place, of course, is Australia. It has a vocabulary as unique as its koalas and kangaroos. If you've always thought Down Under would be a great place to visit because you wouldn't need to learn a foreign language, think again. Australian-English is a foreign language to anyone not born or raised there. The words, not only the accent, are unfamiliar. You might want to learn a few basics before getting embarrassed by a "true Aussie" who won't mind **taking the mickey out** of a Yank, or trying to order take-out food. Learning the spoken variations is fun because Australians cannot be serious about a language they've enjoyed molding with their clever tongues.

First, the basics: The word *Australians* is a long one—so, Australians, along with the rest of the world, call themselves **Aussies,** pronounced with a "zz" sound." (When reading the alphabet, *Z* is called "zed." In words, the pronunciation does not change.) *Australia*, too, is a long word, so in recent years Australians have adopted a fairy-tale nickname for their homeland—**OZ** (which stresses the "z.") Maybe Australia is not the mythical Oz which Dorothy and Toto searched for, but it's about as far away from Kansas as you can get.

These are just a few examples of how Australians constantly shorten words. Some critics would call it laziness and others might see it as individualism. Whatever the reason, Aussies have created a secondary vocabulary of stunted words for everyday speech. Sometimes that makes it hard to keep up with a conversation. Try working through these snippets: Grown men pack up their **tinnies** and head for the **footy.** When they get to the **footy grounds** they look for the best

22

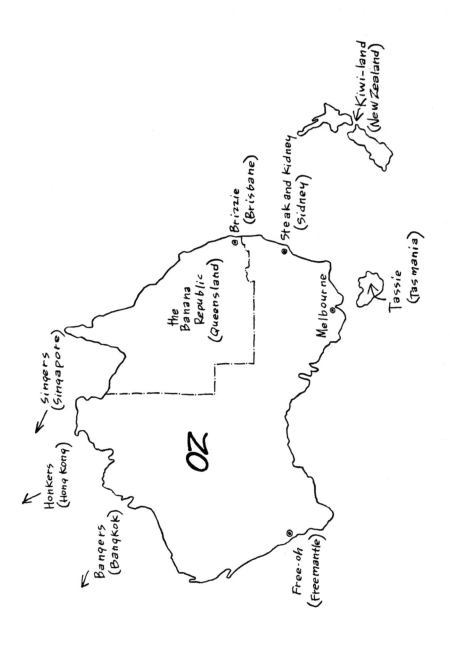

Kiwi-land
(New Zealand)

Steak and kidney
(Sidney)

Brizzie
(Brisbane)

the
Banana
Republic
(Queensland)

Tassie
(Tasmania)

Melbourne

Singers
(Singapore)

OZ

Honkers
(Hong Kong)

Free-oh
(Freemantle)

Bangers
(Bangkok)

possible **possie** (with a "zz" sound), first in the **car park,** then in the stands.

Did you get it? We'll go through it phrase by phrase: **tinnies** are tin cans containing beer (which are no longer made of tin), and **footy** is short for **Australian Rules Football** or **Aussie Rules.** Footy is neither soccer nor rugby, and Australia is the only country in which it is played. **Possie** (or **pozzie**) is the colloquial abbreviation of *position*—a word used more frequently by Australians than Americans. It takes the place of *space* or *spot,* as in "Find me a space" or "Save me a spot." Instead, it's **"Get me a pozzie."** By the way, **car park** substitutes for parking lot.

From the moment Australians get up in the morning they clip their words. The first meal of the day is **brekky** when they may drink tea with **bickies,** otherwise known as **biscuits,** which are really crackers or cookies. (More about that in the food section.) A newspaper might even feature a listing for "The Best Brekky in Town." In New York, they would write about places for brunch!

Even holidays aren't sacred. In general, the Christmas season is referred to as **the hollies,** a time when you may escape to a **holly house** to get away from the city. Of course, only the upper and upper-middle crusts can afford a holiday retreat. Whether away for the holidays or not, everyone hopes to get **prezzies** (presents) for **Chrissy.** Yes, it's true. Perhaps with Christmas in the summer, some of the formality is taken out of the holiday. That may account for it being called **Chrissy.** (Perhaps you didn't realize that the seasons are different in Northern and Southern hemispheres. So a U.S. winter is an Aussie summer.)

Children and adults wait for **prezzies** from their friends and relatives, known as the **rellies** or **relos.** The

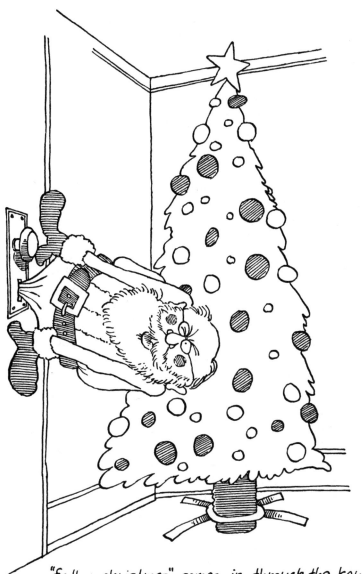

"father christmas" comes in through the keyhole!

little ones leave their pillow slips (cases) out on Christmas Eve hoping **Father Christmas** will fill them with gifts. After all, why worry about stockings in the summer? While **Father Christmas** remains common, most children know him as Santa, too. By any name, he's the guy in the red suit carrying all the presents. But, because most of Australia has a hot climate and kids don't have chimneys in their houses, they know Santa gets into their homes in a different way—he magically comes through the keyhole.

Another holiday tradition often bows to the hot weather: the English roast dinner complete with plum pudding on Christmas Day. Now many Aussie families invite friends to a **barby** in the **arvo** instead. That translates into a barbecue in the afternoon. If you lived in a climate where it could be 105° Fahrenheit on Christmas, you'd think twice about turning on the oven, too. Despite the distance from England in time and miles, Aussies hold onto some of the quaint British customs, like party hats for the children at Christmas (not on New Year's Eve) and pulling **crackers** or **bon bons** for fun. The **crackers** are not food or firecrackers. They are those paper party favors that pop! **Bon bons** are another name for **crackers.**

After high school, students can go on for tertiary education at the **the uni,** or university. **Uni students** attend classes there, not co-eds or college kids. Children who live too far away from any school to attend in person must rely on state-run correspondence classes. The **postie** (postman) delivers schoolwork to those known as **corro students.** The media go a long way to sustain the colloquialized language. One series of articles on education carried headlines such as: "When School Is Carried in the Postie's Bag" and "Loneliness of Corro Kids." It's a headline editor's dream come true—abbreviations everyone understands. You might think some of these phrases are jargon, unique to particular trades, but they are not.

Like **postie** for mailman, many other occupations have been retitled. Journalists are **journos.** Broadcast **journos** make **doccos** (documentaries) for **telly** (television). Politicians answer to **pollies**; environmentalists and conservationists know everyone calls them **greenies**; truck drivers are **truckies** (not truckers). In the motorcycle world, two stunted words have different meanings: **bikers** (same as the American word) ride motorcycles. **Bikies,** belong to motorcycle gangs!

Trammies (would you believe adults wear that as a moniker?) drive trams in Melbourne and Adelaide where they still have the trolley-like system. The milkman gets tagged **milko** (or **"milk-oh"**). In the same vein, a bricklayer is a **brickie,** and a bottle collector, who was a busy man before plastic disposables, was politely called a **bottle-oh.** A **garbo** collects garbage. By the way, **ambos** drive ambulances. The list does not end there. Other occupations have titles which do not resemble anything spoken in the U.S.A. We will get to those later.

Rhyming Slang

The second colorful derivation of the Queen's English employed Down Under is **rhyming slang.** The cockney convicts transported to the 18th-century penal colony, which would become the country of Australia, brought with them this barbarism of the spoken tongue. The cockneyisms are not used constantly but they do slip into conversations often enough to merit explanation. It should be noted that the Aussies adopted the practice of creating descriptive rhymes and from them developed new phrases that no cockney would recognize as his own.

To get on with working this out: **trouble and strife** means *wife*—not very flattering, but heard all the time. In the same spirit, **cheese and kisses** means *Mrs.* and a **china plate** is your mate or spouse. **Billy lids** are kids. (A **billy** is a pot in which to boil water, among other things. More on that later.)

A **hollow log** is a dog and a **ballarat** creeps into conversation as a cat! **Ballarat** is a rural city not far from Melbourne—it is not unusual for place names to sneak into the rhyme scheme. An **Oxford scholar** is not a person. **Scholar** rhymes with *dollar*. At closing time in the vegetable market one day, a greengrocer might shout, "Two **caulies** for an **Oxford!**" He is selling two heads of cauliflower for a dollar—not a bad deal!

The phrase **Warwick Farms** (a suburb of Sydney, pronounced "WAR-rick") substitutes for *arms*, which rhymes with *farms*; and **under the Warwicks** has come to mean underarms. You may have noted that once the rhymes themselves become familiar, they, too, get shortened, as in **Oxford** for *dollar* and **under the Warwicks** for *underarms*. It is understood generally that **Warwicks** refers to **Warwick Farms** and **farms** is the catchword here. **Trouble under the Warwicks** denotes a euphemism to let you know it's time for a **plastic** or a **plastic flower. Flower** rhymes with shower!

Just as places can be used to make a rhyme, they can be the object of the rhyme as well. You may hear someone say, "I'll be in **Steak and Kidney** by morning." If you remember **Kidney** is the rhyming word, you'll realize they mean *Sydney*.

Another time you may be asked, "How's your **hol-**

cockney rhyming slang
trouble and strife = wife

low?" "My hollow what?" is a legitimate reaction. This time, recall **hollow log** rhymes with dog. Now, you are ahead of the game. A pet lover may have a **hollow** and a **ballarat** living in the house at the same time!

"Pick up the **Al Capone**" or "answer the **eau de cologne**" both tell you to answer the telephone. If you're told to wear a **bag of fruit,** don't be insulted. It's only a suit. And if you would like to top it off properly you'll don a **tit-for-tat,** or more commonly called a **tit-for. Tat** rhymes with *hat* and that's what the occasion calls for.

When taking a **Captain Cook** you simply take a look, and a **babbling brook** stands for *cook.* How do you know which is which? The Aussies will say you just know! They learn it and commit it to memory without trying, just like the alphabet or their first words.

Sometimes in rhyming slang the context changes the meaning. Just as Captain Cook and Al Capone have gotten into the act, so has **Bob Hope.** This comedian takes the place of either *soap* or *dope* (as in *drugs).* I wonder if he knows that? Sometimes **Bob Hope** will be found soaking beneath a **plastic flower;** but at other times the people who deal or abuse **Bob Hope** may run into **John Hop.** He's the guy on the beat, dressed in blue, ready to throw the **crim** (criminal) into the **divvy van** and drive away. The **divvy van** belongs to the divisional police headquarters and is the equivalent of a paddy wagon. (Of course, "paddy wagon" is considered U.S. slang, a phrase with it's own colorful etymology.)

If you run away from **the johns** (the pared down version of **John Hops** or cops) you'll be **going it Pat Malone**—going alone! Because of this meaning, *john* is not synonymous with *toilet.*

To add to the minor difficulties you may already be

having, quite a few words in Aussie-English are the same as in American-English, but the pronunciations vary slightly (even if the accents are the same). It may take a moment for the American ear to catch up with the spoken word. Anyone familiar with British-English will find some variations easy enough to comprehend. Most of them were born as old English forms, dropped by Americans generations ago.

These examples should provide you with some understanding: Horseracing tops the list as Australia's number one spectator sport, a true national pastime that is rivaled only by cricket. **The Melbourne Cup,** raced in November every year (in Melbourne obviously) remains big news on the social scene as well as for the racehorse investors and **punters** (bettors). It's the Aussie version of England's Ascot. But, any **darby,** no matter how small or local, creates excitement whenever or wherever it takes place. **Darby?** They spell it "derby," as in the Kentucky Derby, but the e is pronounced "a", hence, **darby. Clerk** follows the same logic. They say "clark."

American trains run on or close to schedule with a "sked" sound in it. But the Aussies talk about train schedules with a "shed" sound. So no one will ever ask for a train sked. Another familiar word which sounds different is *jaguar.* While the American name of the animal only has two syllables, the Aussies have lengthened the sound to "jag-gu-aahr." Perhaps that makes the luxury car sound more luxurious and the great cat seem more sleek.

A favorite word that causes a bit of consternation is *aluminum.* The British and the Australians say: "al-u-min-nee-um." That's because they spell the word with an extra syllable: **aluminium.** See the "mini" in there!

The American word does not contain that syllable. By the way, the stuff housekeepers wrap leftovers in has been pared down to **al-foil.**

Tyres on the car, *colour, favour, neighbour, harbour* and *labour* keep the British spellings with a notable exception: the Australian Labor Party (ALP)—which is as big as the Republicans or Democrats—spells *labor* the American way. That's the equivalent of naming a product "lite" instead of "light."

When parking a car in Australia, a driver might be surprised when his **tyres** rub the **kerb** until he reads a construction sign explaining: **"kerb realignment in process."** That means the local council has decided to narrow the road to slow drivers down. They alter the **kerb.** Americans would alter the "curb."

Australians employ many other Britishisms constantly throughout their language, too many to name them all. But, let's look at a few more everyday terms which will be familiar to your ear, but not to your eye.

Cheque, as in "traveler's cheque" or "bank cheque," is not a fancier way to spell "check." Instead "cheque" is the correct and only spelling of the monetary substitution in the Queen's English and the banking system run by her subjects. Another example is the elongated version of **tonnes.** It seems like a ton of letters to use for a monosyllabic word, but the Aussies use it to denote the metric **tonne,** which weighs more than the U.S. ton.

If you are expecting a package during a visit Down Under, you may have to pick it up at the **despatch** office of the shipping company. Don't let it throw you. They will dispatch it no matter how you spell it—you hope.

With these basics, most people should start to comprehend and feel comfortable with the fresh and, in many cases, witty words and expressions evolved from the workaday world of The Antipodes. If you've never heard that phrase, let me explain: *Antipodes* is the early mapmakers' reference to Australia, used by the British to describe their colony in the Southern Hemisphere. *Antipodes* stems from the Greek, meaning "on the opposite side of the globe."

Keep in mind, shortened words can describe anything, whether clothing, travel destinations, food, drink or sports, as can rhyming slang. The idioms weave in and out of conversations between mother and child, farmers and white collar workers, and can be heard on television and radio broadcasts. The **pollies** rely on colloquialisms as much as the banker and **milko** do.

The Aussie tongue has few regionalisms. The only divisions in the spoken language are bits of jargon leaning more toward country life than life in the cities. But, in a nation reliant on its farmers and graziers, and where agriculture still dominates most of the land mass, country words find themselves easily understood. In some cases, they've been expanded to take on new citified definitions, but the original meanings are not lost.

Phrases which may seem outdated stay alive lovingly in the nation's ballads and poetry and get passed on to each generation of children and visitors. However, there is one animal stalking the lexicon of Australia which may do more damage than anyone could believe possible—American television. The language that stood as a refreshing reflection of a national character is falling prey to the Cookie Monster and his screen cronies who gobble up the Aussie vocabulary and replace it with Americanisms such as "cookie" and "zee" rather than **biscuit, bickie** or **zed.** Only time will tell if the Aussies fight back with characteristic gusto or if their isolated fortress has fallen too far too fast.

CHAPTER TWO

A Slice of Pavlova, Please?

Food is a universal language. Everyone eats. Food is also personal, protected by pet names in every country. The kind of food eaten reflects the nation's lifestyle, as well as its climate and tradition.

When you talk about food in Australia, you talk about **tucker**. Whether you're asked, "Will ya stay for tucker, Mate?" or hear a television commercial touting a brand of macaroni as "Good Aussie Tucker!", the word will not escape you. **Tucker** is the food of everyday life, not the kind found in gourmet restaurants, but in the kitchens of most homes, at the corner store and at a takeout place.

Historically, tucker was carried on a wagon stored in a **tuckerbox**, an early version of a cooler. But, if a man was traveling on foot or horseback, he'd carry his lunch in a **tuckerbag.** Now, there's a chain of supermarkets calling itself **Tuckerbag.** Very clever!

A **tuckshop** sounds like something a tailor would run; but, Australian school children buy snacks or quick lunches at the **tuckshop** on schoolgrounds. **Mums** even volunteer to staff the **tuckshop** in many schools. It's the equivalent of a snack bar.

When it comes to food Down Under, **vegemite** is the first thing that comes to mind, followed by the great Aussie meat pie.

Vegemite is a blackish salty paste composed of yeast extract produced by Kraft, the cheese food company. At least two generations of Australian **mums** have been convinced that eating Vegemite is good for children. They spread it thinly on toast or crackers and serve it for lunch or breakfast. Kids will ask for Vegemite sandwiches as often as American kids eat peanut butter and jelly. The label is as popular in pop art as the Campbell's soup can once was. It shows up on beach towels, puzzles, posters and greeting cards, as a true symbol of modern Oz.

Somewhere along the way, you might hear the comparative statement: "It's as **dinky-di** Australian as Vegemite." That's about as Australian as apple pie is American. **Dinky-di** substitutes for truly or honestly.

A word of warning: If you weren't brought up on Vegemite you may never acquire a taste for it. In fact, you might never get past the smell!

We've already mentioned that breakfast is called **brekky,** but didn't list what people eat for the first meal of the day. At home, you may have a **cuppa** of white or black tea or coffee. When you accept **white tea** or **white coffee** be prepared to have it served with the milk already in it—and very milky at that!

Other than Vegemite on toast, there's always **jam,** but

never jelly. **Jelly** in Australia is gelatin (like JELLO). **Pikelets** are another option. They are fat doughy silver-dollar-size pancakes. Maple syrup will not be on the menu. (Maple trees are not indigenous to Australia, but maple-flavored syrup is beginning to show up on store shelves, although many Aussies are not sure what to use it for.) Their sweet breakfast topping is **golden syrup** or **treacle,** a syrup made during the refining of sugar cane. Cane farming is a major industry in the Sunshine State of Queensland.

Aussies enjoy dry cereals, too. After all they grow lots of wheat and grain. High-fiber eaters will find granola hiding on store shelves behind packaging marked **muesli.** Commercially marketed cereals bear similar names to their U.S. cousins, but one popular brandname doesn't ring true to American ears: Rice krispies are sold as **rice bubbles.**

Often a motel will leave tea or coffee and **biscuits** or **bickies** for a quick breakfast. Do not think of biscuits as the dinner rolls Americans butter up. **Dry biscuits** or **dry bickies** are crackers and **sweet biscuits** or **sweet bickies** are cookies. Cookies only became known in Australia with the onslaught of the Cookie Monster of *Sesame Street.*

Scones look and taste like American biscuits. They're usually offered at morning tea, for a coffee break, or afternoon tea, following the British custom of tea at three or four o'clock.

Aussies like English muffins but they like **crumpets** even more. American-style muffins cannot be found by that name in Australia. They call baked goods which resemble muffins **little cakes** and they usually serve them the same way—with butter.

The Australians often sit down to a British Devonshire tea, too, which seems incongruous with most of the Australian climate. The Devonshire tea is offered most commonly during afternoon teatime. During **devvy tea** (keep it short), you are treated to a pot of tea and hot doughy scones with thick fresh cream and jam lobbed on top of them. It seems fitting to have such a treat on a gray, rainy London afternoon, but not in Australia. Imagine this: You find yourself driving through the tropics of Queensland when you pass **tea rooms,** advertising Devonshire tea. It's 100° Fahrenheit in the shade (about 37° Celsius) and you're sweltering. It does not seem right to sit down to a hot treat of any kind. But people do!

In blistering heat, for which most of Australia is known, an American would look for a tall iced tea to quench his thirst. He can search all he wants, he'll probably never find it, and he'll get some strange looks along the way. I once got a cup of hot tea when I unknowingly asked for iced tea, and when I thought the waitress had misunderstood, I repeated my request for some ice in the tea. The next thing I knew, a saucer with a few ice cubes was plunked down beside my teacup and the waitress walked away mumbling something unflattering under her breath. My traveling companion looked at me like I was crazy. Even when I explained, the look remained quizzical.

I must admit I did find Twinings instant tea once in a supermarket gourmet section which had directions for iced tea on the package, but I doubt any Aussie shopper ever bothered to read the label. Even if they did, they probably wouldn't take the suggestion seriously.

Do not despair. You can get **iced coffee,** but the price on most menus will surprise you—about twice what you would expect to pay in an American deli, because it's not simply not strong coffee with milk over ice. No! They fill the biggest glass they can find with milky coffee and then throw in a scoop of ice cream and plop whipped cream on top. So delightful, but it is more a dessert than a beverage.

On breakfast menus in **roadhouses** (diners) or **coffee lounges** (luncheonettes), two strange selections may be found—strange to Yanks: **spaghetti on toast** and **baked beans on toast.** Baked beans seldom show up any other way. They're the canned variety made with tomato sauce rather than Boston-style, baked with molasses. I've never tried either the **spags** or **beans on toast** for **brekky.** I don't know any Americans who have!

Sandwiches, the mainstays of lunch Down Under, too, stack up a bit thinner than most American ones. **Sangers** consist of a sliver of meat or cheese or tomato or **beetroot** (red beets) between two slices of amply buttered **roses are red** or toast. **Roses are red** rhymes with bread. So, "butter up some **roses!**" Because of their small size, people order a plate of mixed sandwiches. They remind me of the tea sandwiches or finger sandwiches Aunt Bea made for Ladies' Club luncheons.

A fancier kind of toasted sanger is a **jaffle.** The **jaffle** gets buttered on the outside as well as the inside and it's placed between two hotplates inside the **jaffle iron,** which works like a waffle iron. Most people put cheese on a jaffle so it melts. You'll even find sprouts and other exotica on modern jaffles.

For lunch on the run, or any other meal for that matter, **takeaway** shops abound—that's takeout under an assumed name. There you'll pick up some of the fast foods that helped color the Australian character long before McDonald's and Kentucky Fried Chicken arrived.

A **meat pie** equals a personal-size pot pie, traditionally filled with ground beef and a spicy brown

spaghetti on toast

gravy. They eat **pies** smothered in **sauce** (or **dead horse** in rhyming slang). **Sauce** is ketchup, or catsup—short for **tomato sauce.** Since tomato sauce comes out of a ketchup bottle, they douse pasta with spaghetti sauce, red sauce or marinara sauce. Aussies like Worcestershire sauce but refer to it as **black sauce,** not to be confused with Chinese black bean sauce.

One other grab-on-the-run lunch is **pie and peas**— just that—a meat pie with a lump of green peas on top, with or without sauce. If pies don't steal your fancy, a few other quickie bites line up in the **pie warmer** next to them: **sausage rolls, pasties,** and **chiko rolls.** Sausage rolls are **minced** (ground up) sausage meat wrapped in pastry, fried, then kept warm for takeaway. **Pasties** ("pah-sties") are flaky crust pastry pockets filled with mashed vegetables. **Chiko rolls** and **spring rolls** are Aussie versions of Chinese egg rolls. "Chiko" is a brand name for mass-marketed versions found at most takeaway shops.

Dim sims, another Chinese delicacy popularized in Oz, are bite-sized meat pieces wrapped in dough and either fried or steamed. They call **dim sims** "dim sum selections" in U.S. Chinese restaurants, but in Australia, they can be bought in just about any snack bar.

Australians consider **milk bars** their unique phenomena. But urban Yanks see them as the equal of the corner grocery, *bodega* or mom-and-pop-shop (lost to suburbia). They stock milk, eggs and other necessities. The only difference between the U.S. store and the Aussie **bar** is that most **milk bars** have grills to make hamburgers, or fish and chips and a pie warmer. Of course, old-fashioned **cut sandwiches** can be found too.

Hot dogs in milk bars or anywhere else have many pseudonyms: **Saveloys** or **savs** take their name from a popular brand. A **dagwood dog** is a frank stuck on a long stick, coated in batter and deep fried. Before eating it, you smother it in sauce. You buy **dagwoods** at outdoor fetes (pronounced "fates" in Oz) from food stands or vending trucks. You won't find Dagwood-style club sandwiches anywhere.

In a country that loves the ocean and all its bounty, you'd expect to find **fish and chips.** And you do. The street staple is as commonplace there as in Britain. **Chips** does not mean potato chips. They look like fat french fries. American-style fries came in with McDonalds. The **fish** can be any kind of **fillet** (that's *filet* with the T pronounced). Often **flake** numbers among the fish choices. **Flake** is shark meat. Usually you can order your fish breaded and fried or **grilled. Grilling** in this case is broiling, not barbecuing. Home kitchens have **grillers,** not broilers, in their ovens.

At the beach, where takeaway beats carrying a heavy cooler all day, the gourmet fast food eater may choose **prawn cutlets**, a batter-dipped, fried butterflied shrimp. Make sure the frozen variety get fully thawed before they deep fry them or you'll wind up donating lunch to the eager seagulls flocking around you.

Sausages show up everywhere—at breakfast, lunch and supper and particularly at **barbies**—the only name for Australian barbecues. In the slang nomenclature, sausages bear the nicknames **bangers** and **snags. Bangers** is another British-English term, commonly heard in the food phrase **bangers and mash,** or sausages and potatoes.

Alas, in recent history, American fast food has begun to compete strongly with Aussie takeaway. Kentucky Fried Chicken encroached first, then McDonald's and Burger King arrived under the *nom de plume* **Happy Jack's.** The primary dissimilarity between McDonald's

U.S. and Australian can be found in the advertising. While American ads push the wholesome all-American-kids-style, the Aussie company promotes its "Australian-ness." One commercial jingle sings the praises of pure Aussie beef and Tasmanian potatoes. (Tasmania is one of Australia's six states.) I suppose it would be too expensive to import potatoes from Idaho and Maine.

Thirsting for lemonade? Think again. It will be as hard to find as iced tea. **Lemonade** in Australia means lemon soda, a carbonated beverage like 7UP. The word **soda** by itself denotes soda water only. Australians never use the term *club soda*. Flavored carbonated drinks of all kinds are **soft drinks.** Coke is Coke, just about anywhere. If you don't want a carbonated soft drink, you may wind up with a **cordial.** No, not the liqueur, but "cor-dee-al," a liquid version of KOOL-AID. Cordials are thick concentrated fruit flavorings mixed with water in your own kitchen. The most recent rage is to mix cordials with naturally carbonated mineral water. Rather chic!

Once you're done with lunch and afternoon tea is over, it's time to think about supper. When visiting someone's home you may be invited to stay for **tea**—that means dinner—not to be confused with the other teatimes during the day.

After this invitation, your host or hostess may say, "I hope you don't mind **bubble and squeak** tonight." In Oz, the cook is apologizing for serving leftovers (though rarely would guests get anything out of **al-foil** for **tea,** except in a pinch.)

One of the vegetables on the table may be **pumpkin.** "No," you say. You make pies out of pumpkin, not a side dish. But in Oz, **pumpkin** describes the same **veggie** we call squash, as in **butternut pumpkin.** If you asked for **squash,** you'd get a beverage—a thick pulpy lemon or orange soda poured over crushed ice. So ask for **squash** instead of 7UP, and ask for **pumpkin** instead of squash, and if you're in dire need of pumpkin pie, you'd better go back to the States.

A number of other vegetable names can throw you, too. Red beets are **beetroot,** and as we said earlier, are commonly found sliced up on sandwiches. **Silverbeet** is similar to Swiss chard. Broccoli can be pronounced "brock-col-EYE." If a vegetable or any other food has been in the refrigerator too long, you might notice it's **on the nose,** or **gone off,** which all means it has turned bad and stinks!

Like opposing camps, food breaks down into two distinct tastes in Australia: **sweet** or **savory. Sweet** can be anything candyish, fruity or creamy. **Savory** is just the opposite: anything not sweet, including paté, asparagus, cheese dips, cheese, etc. The word **sweets** by itself generally means desserts and **savories** are canapés or hors d'oeuvres. Again, meaning depends on context.

After dinner you'll be offered sweets with your coffee or tea. **Pavlova** numbers among the favorites. **Pav** resembles a meringue-type dessert made of whipped egg whites and **heaps** of sugar. A **lamington** or **lam** is a small square sponge cake with shredded coconut all over it. The ever-loved **bickie** may show up on a plate once again. Any sweets may prove **moreish,** meaning they'll make you want more of them!

One particular treat is an **Anzac** biscuit. It's the Aussie version of an oatmeal cookie. **Anzacs** combine wheat flour, rolled oats, shredded coconut and golden syrup. History shows they were homemade goods sent overseas to the troops, or **Anzacs,** during the First World War. A.N.Z.A.C. is an acronym for the Australian and New Zealand Army Corps who fought for the British Empire. We'll talk more about them later.

If you've gone to a movie with the kids and decide to go for a snack afterwards, a very special treat will be a **spider!** Spiders are like ice cream sodas or floats, made with flavorings, soda water and ice cream.

Children also like **lollies,** not candy. **Boiled lollies** are hard candy in general; **fairy floss** is cotton candy and Aussies call chewing gum **chewie,** never gum. **"Can I bot a chewie?"** was the first uniquely Australian phrase I ever heard and didn't understand. The asker meant, "Can I borrow (with no intention of returning) a piece of gum?" In that sense, you can **bot** anything; and someone who does it all the time is known as **a bot.**

While we're on the subject of chewing gum, it might interest you to learn that Wrigley's brand gum, like Juicy Fruit, isn't sold in sticks, rather as candy-coated chiclet-type things which the makers call **pellets.** Most people call them "pieces." What will surprise a stranger in Oz is that they sell pellets in the same size and shape packages as a five-stick or seven-stick pack of gum. When you open it, you'll be surprised to find the candy-coated pieces inside.

Just as Hershey markets itself as "The great American chocolate bar," there are many brand names Down Under synonymous with Aussie childhood. Among them are **Violet Crumble, Jaffas, Smarties** (similar to M&Ms), **Cherry Ripes** and **Minties.** Chocolate, by itself, falls victim to the stunted vocabulary—usually melted down to **chockie.** Hence, even an adult may find himself tempted by a **chockie bickie** or **chockie syrup** on ice cream.

For truly fancy fare, Australians look to numerous seafood restaurants, numerous because all the major cities are port towns. The names of the delicacies have

been changed but the tastes have not. Starting at the top of the range: A lobster is a **crayfish.** You're probably wondering if lobsters are called **crayfish,** what are crayfish called? They are **yabbies.** Some of the nicest **yabbies** I know grow up in the Murray River between the states of New South Wales and Victoria. They are trapped and taken to local restaurants where they are lightly barbecued to perfection.

Another edible and delectable crustacean from the sea not heard of in America is the **bay bug.** Formal names for **bug** are **Balmain bug** and **Moreton Bay bug.** While it may not sound scrumptious, the **bug** is delicious. The longer names tell diners where the **bug** was caught. **Balmain** is a Sydney suburb on Sydney Harbour. Further north, fishermen trap bugs in Moreton Bay off Brisbane. Both are varieties of bay lobsters or shovel-nosed lobsters, differentiated that way only by fishermen and scientists. Some gourmet palates claim the Balmain bug has a more natural garlicky flavor than its Queensland (the state where Brisbane and Moreton Bay are located) **rellie** (relative). On a plate, bugs resemble small lobster tails split in half—you eat mostly the tail of the bug. Their bodies are very small and they have no claws to speak of.

Not to be left out, we'll throw another **prawn** on the **barby. Prawn?** They call all shrimp **prawns,** regardless of size or origin. But if you want to be impressed by size and flavor, ask for a **king prawn** or **tiger prawn.** They're so big you would never consider calling them "shrimp."

While food has different names on Aussie menus, the menus are laid out differently too. The use of the word **entree** regularly confuses Americans. The Aussies use the term correctly, as opposed to U.S. restauranteurs. *Entree* has the connotation of "upon entering" or

"first." So, your first choice on the menu Down Under should be an **entree. Appetisers** usually head the column of soups and salads. After them comes the **main course,** which is usually called the *entree* in America. Often seafood dishes or pasta can be ordered in either main-size or entree-size portions. Remember, the entree is smaller.

When sitting down for a long leisurely dinner, you may not want to rush right into dessert, but rather wish to finish your wine with more savory tastes before choosing coffee and sweets. In that case, you may order **cheese and greens.** It's basically a cheese-and-crackers plate with a bit of fresh fruit or vegetable accompanying it.

The Pub

Drinking is an important part of life in Oz and the **pub** is a subculture in this land of long hot summers. **Pubs** and **hotels** are interchangeable words in most cases, dating back to the old laws (most of which still exist), which commanded any establishment selling liquor to provide food and accommodation as well. Pubs are found everywhere—city, country, back streets and main roads.

In rhyming slang the pub is a **rub-a-dub,** a **rubbity-dub** or just a **rubbity.** Rhyming slang is used a lot in pubs where drink loosens the tongue. Pubs have always been male domain. That's not to say women cannot drink in a pub, but the pub is male oriented. It is a place where men hit the **turps** (any alcohol, a shortened form of *turpentine*), mainly **pig's ear** (rhymes with beer); where another man might swill **aunty's downfall** or **mother's sin** (both terms for gin); and yet another may sip a bit of **plonk** or **bombo,** which rank as generic terms for any cheap cask wine.

Ordering beer is an art. You might order a **pony,** a **middy,** a **pot** or a **schooner,** but that has nothing to do with the kind of beer you intend to drink. It reflects the size of the glass you intend to down. The names differ among the states. A **schooner** is a 15-ounce glass. (The ounce is a throwback to before Australia went metric.) A **middy** equals ten ounces in New South Wales, and a **pot** means the smaller size in other states. A regular glass gets called a **glass,** filled with seven ounces of beer. The tiniest glass, not often found, is the **pony,** filled with only five ounces.

To bounce from pub to pub in a given night is to do **the pub crawl,** the Aussie version of "bar hopping." And if you intend to party hearty all night long, you and your friends are out for a **rage** or gone **raging.** The expression the next morning might be, "I've got a hangover. We **raged** all night."

The guy who buys the round announces: "It's my **shout.**" or in rhyming slang, he might insist on his **wally grout.** The phrase gets stretched in other ways. If friends intend to treat someone to lunch for a birthday, they will **shout** them lunch.

You can, of course, have lunch in a pub. Usually you order from a blackboard menu, pay up front at a counter and get served by a waiter or waitress. According to tradition, pubs serve lunch strictly between the hours of noon and two P.M. Not a moment later. They serve dinner between six and eight. In some areas that's changing, but when traveling, it's better to be safe than sorry. After all, the pub may be the only **fang** (food) in town.

Fang is another silly word. It probably stems from *fang* meaning "tooth" and having to do with mouth and eating. When friends get together and decide to go for a bite to eat, someone might say, "Let's **grab a fang.**"

Australians enjoy eating out. In Melbourne, **B.Y.O.** restaurants are popular. That's where you can bring your own wine or beer. On a weekend, you may find it hard to get into a place without booking a table ahead. Popular eateries are **chock-a-block** or **chocker.** That means chock-full or packed to the rafters.

Delis have become popular in Australian cities, particularly gourmet deli/restaurants. They claim to be a takeoff on New York delis, but I'm afraid they are a bit too **flash** or **swish** (fancy) for that. In Melbourne alone, I've run into three restaurants with New York names: The New York Deli, Café Manhattan and The Wall Street Deli.

One delicatessen delicacy not to be found Down Under is the corned-beef sandwich. The closest thing you will find is **silverside.** Then again, why would anyone travel ten thousand miles to look for something they can have in their own backyard?

CHAPTER THREE

What's a Mate?

"Can I bot a chewie, **mate**?" "Cheers, **mate**!" "Whose **mate** is that?" "Bring your **mates** along." That's Bobby's little **mate**." All these sentences have one thing in common, the word **mate**. It's heard constantly throughout Australia. But what is a **mate**?

A **mate** is the masculine synonym for friend, a buddy or pal. He could be a close co-worker, companion, teammate or neighbor. A father will call his son **mate**, a grandfather his grandson, an uncle his nephew. **Mate** is a catchy, warm, friendly phrase that men cannot help using. They've heard it all their lives and newcomers find it as comfortable as an old glove.

It's a compliment for one man to refer to another as "a **mate of mine**." The fellow has been singled out as a good and true friend by this male endearment in its most fundamental form. **Best mates** is the highest plateau of comraderie or **mateship** among Australian males. Little boys have their best **mates** and adults do too. "I'm going to the **footy** with my **mates** on Saturday," means the fellow is going with a close circle of friends, his best buddies.

While a mother may distinguish her son as "mate" (perhaps readying the boy for the male world) most men do not like and do not expect to be referred to as "mate" by a woman. Mark that unacceptable! However, in recent years, more women co-workers characterize their male counterparts as "mates," in general. But, hearing a woman say, "Thanks, mate," will bring a scowl to most men's faces! It's just **not on** (not the way things are done)! She could get away with it in jest or sarcastically. Then, of course, everything is fair game.

Mate works as a generic label, as well, for the male stranger behind the store counter or for the man you've just been introduced to. It becomes a polite form of address, man to man. "How much for the sanger, **mate?**" Or when used in anger it sounds similar to a truck driver shouting: "Look, Mac, get off the road!" Substitute **mate** for *Mac*.

Digger can replace *mate* in conversation, though not frequently. The history of **digger** commands more interest. A digger was a miner who dug up the earth during the Australian gold rush of the 1850s. The digger's hardworking wife was a **diggeress.** (Yuk!) Later, during World War One, the Aussie foot soldiers were renamed **diggers** during their service in the trenches fighting for Mother England. Once again Australians were carrying shovels but for an updated reason. Those **khaki-clad** (pronounced "car-key") soldiers were the **Anzacs,** members of the Australian and New Zealand Army Corps. The **Anzacs** were the men in the **slouch hats** or **slouchies.** The hat has one side of the brim pinned up so it doesn't get in the way of the rifle carried over the soldier's shoulder. The **slouch** has become synonymous with Australia the world over.

Cobber can substitute for either **digger** or **mate,** but gets used even less frequently. Any man is a **bloke,** a fellow, a guy. But any bloke can be **Fred** or **Norm**—your average Aussie man. Fred or Norm star in most jokes too. Even a nationwide public service fitness campaign starred a cartoon character named Norm. He was the epitome of the beer-swilling, overweight armchair athlete, and his presence has added Norm to the vocabulary, always meaning that hard-drinking, non-exercising bloke.

When the answer to a question goes beyond obvious, the sarcastic response involves **Fred:** "Even **Blind Freddy** can see that!" Anyone could understand it, or know it, whatever *it* is!

On the same linguistic track, a woman is a **sheila.** While **sheila** does not flatter a woman, the name doesn't really degrade her either. It has a particular place in conversation, used only by men in reference to women. A woman would never characterize her friends as **sheilas.** Members of the female sex from teen-agers on up may be referred to as **birds.** It's not too different from using *chick* to describe a woman, but it's spoken more often.

Meantime, a little girl falls prey to rhyming slang in the phrase **Barossa pearl.** The rhyme stems from the Barossa Valley, a verdant wine-making region in the state of South Australia. As is their habit, the Aussies will clip the slang phrase and **barossa** alone becomes synonymous with girl.

Most Americans associate Australia with the song "Waltzing Matilda." The ballad tells the tale of the **swagman,** a central figure in Australian lore. The **swag-**

man is the paragon of the independent spirit of the Land Down Under, the stuff of which legends are made. A **swagman** or a **swaggie** was marked by the bedroll or **swag** carried on his back, from which he takes his name.

The **swaggie** was an itinerant who roamed the **outback** on foot in search of an occasional day's work in a town or on a **station** (ranch) and worked for bed and board. Sometimes his **swag** was a **bluey** because the blankets were made of blue wool. To **hump bluey** means to sling a bedroll across your back. The swag or bluey also went by a more affectionate name— **Matilda**—the lady he waltzed with throughout his dusty travels. To lead such a life was **to swag it!**

A **sundowner** was the swaggie who arrived at sunset too late to do a day's work but hoped for **tea** and lodging anyway. Asking for a place to sleep was labeled **backslanging.** Another meaning of **sundowner** refers to men who worked a long day on the property and didn't return until sunset.

Like the swagman, farm life contributes to the strong spoken fabric Down Under. Generally, farmers accept the title **cockies**—once a derogatory term, now not so.

It began with the beautiful white bird with the yellow crest, the **cockatoo.** While bird enthusiasts in America actively seek out cockatoos as exotic pets (remember the one in the *Baretta* television series?), in Australia they live in flocks flying above city rooftops or above the countryside at planting time. When a flock descends on a field, the cockatoos scratch around for seeds to eat. So farmers who tilled the often dry land were dubbed **cockatoos** or **cockies.** Doesn't that make good sense?

From there, as words go in Oz, the definition's perimeter increased to encompass any **man-on-the-land.** A

cow-cocky is a dairy farmer; a **sheep-cocky,** a sheep rancher; a **cane cocky,** a sugar cane plantation owner. The **boss cocky** is the landowner who has men working for him. **Weekend cockies** are city slickers who own small plots of land as second homes. These uses led to the development of the obscure verb **to cocka-too,** meaning "to farm."

One of the fancier terms used with a farmer's name is **pastoralist,** a man who runs sheep, and sometimes cattle or horses, in a large pastoral setting. But most such men on the land would rather be known as **graziers.** The owner of a small block of land gets reduced to a **blockie.**

A **jackeroo** (or **jackaroo**) is not an animal as you might think. He is the apprentice on the station. Now, there's even a four-wheel-drive vehicle with the same name.

The **bushie** or **bushman** spends his life in the outback or the **bush** (which is anywhere outside the cities). The **bushcook** serving the outback drovers on their long rides is the **snag,** just like all the sausages or **snags** he prepares. The rhyming substitution for cook is **babbling brook.**

Every country has its *bandido.* The **bushranger** belongs to Australia. Ned Kelly, in particular, looms as large in legend as Jesse James does. Kelly created a peculiar sensation in his last stand against police by wearing a suit of armor made of discarded tin.

Any bad person is a **baddie,** the opposite of a "goody-goody." But, he may win the title **a bat lot** too—much like a bad penny. While **baddie** can be easily understood, many other "people words" can be more difficult to understand, a favorite being **ocker**—as in "He's just a bloody **ocker!**" You would describe this bloke as an unrefined Australian, a redneck or an embarrassing loud mouth! Norm, the cartoon character with a tinny in his hand, conjures up the big fat ocker at his worst.

Right up there with the local ockers are the other loudmouthed rowdies: the **hoons** and the **larrikans.** Most often these insulting names befit young men who do foolish things for attention. They're blokes who rev car engines and squeal **tyres** outside the pub for the sake of being noticed. You know the type.

In some parts of the country, however, a **hoon** specifically is a man who lives off prostitutes' money; but that's an obscure definition. It proves that usage and context form an important partnership in Aussie colloquial speech.

A **bludger** can fit this second less common meaning of **hoon** as well, according to the dictionary. But, generally a **bludger** won't pull his own weight. The bludger could be the fellow who watches his mates build a barbecue without ever laying a brick and expects to eat from it later. They'll complain, "That bludger will use this barby over my dead body!" Or they might say, at their most colorful, "That bludger **wouldn't work in an iron lung!**" (Where he would'tt even have to breathe!)

Someone singled out for being **on the dole** (the government welfare roles) for no good reason becomes a **dole-bludger.**

A **bodgie** once was considered a worthless person, but, in the 1950s, the name transferred to a group of "greasers" who proudly wore the emblem.

Monosyllabic words seem to reign in this section and that suits the Aussies. A **bab** babbles on and on. A **poon** lives like a hermit in a remote area, often considered a fool because he is naive or unworldly to the point of hurting himself. A **berk** or a **nark** labels a thoroughly unpleasant person, someone to stay as far away from as possible.

Much sweat has been expelled coining words that berate people as stupid or lazy, so the nomenclature continues in its whimsical manner. Because **dilly** rhymes with *silly* it has the identical meaning. Somehow from that beginning the Australians adopted **dills** or **dillpots** as substitutions for *dummy*. **Blinky Bill** rhymes with **dill** and conveys the same idea, too. The real Blinky Bill is an Australian storybook character, a mischievous koala who always **gets into strife** (another expression Aussies use more than Americans.).

Under **dill** include **bunny** (as in *dumb bunny*) and **drongo**. The first slow-witted **drongo** was a race horse by that name in the 1920s who had a penchant for coming in last. Now, **drongo** defines anyone considered slow to catch on, in tribute to that dumb horse.

Pimp in Australia is not what you're thinking. A **pimp** is a tattletale. When you're tattling on someone you're **pimping** on them, as children do. In that sense, it wouldn't be unheard of for a child to cry, "Mummy, Joey's a **pimp!**"—it might be startling to an American.

Because of their height or lack of it, a small child unaffectionately gets tagged an **anklebiter** and pre-school and primary grades are **anklebiter schools.** You see, the cutting tongue spares no one in any sector of society.

Camp describes a homosexual man who must put up with being called a **poofter** or a **poof** behind his back. A lesbian must bear with **lesbo.**

De factos cohabit in a de facto marriage. The one-time Latin legal adjective now shows up daily in newspaper articles, general conversation and insurance policies. **De factos** replaces the terms *live-in boyfriend/girlfriend* or *commonlaw spouse*.

Off to other topics. The stuck-up fellow described as a "stuffed shirt" exudes the same attitude as a **boiled**

shirt. A teller of tall tales has been dubbed a **bommerang bender** and someone who "talks your ear off" has been renamed an **earbasher.** Following that line, a preacher might be rebuffed as a **bible-basher,** charged with **bible-bashing,** presumably because he **bashes** your ear with the Bible's teachings.

The Australian "wordcutters" have carved a few phrases for Christian denominations in addition to the preacher. A Baptist is a **Bappo** and a **Congo** suits a Congregationalist. On that theme: **Metho, Presbo** and **Catho** are Methodists, Presbyterians and Catholics, respectively (but not certainly not respectfully). Other disrespectful but harmless nicknames are **pressbutton** for Presbyterian; and, because most of the early Roman Catholics in Australia were Irish, they were tagged **micks** or **tykes,** also slang for the Irish. The various denominations may not like their nicknames but they're not used to be cruel, just to add variety to the language.

While many occupations have been mentioned already, countless more have been redrawn by Australia's verbal draftsmen. Note this oddity: **zambuck.** The zambuck is an ambulance worker **(ambo)** or emergency first-aid person. But the first connotation specifically belonged to the Saint John's Ambulance Corps attendants, garbed in black-and-white uniforms. Folks at football games especially said the attendants resembled the familiar black-and-white tube of Zambuck first-aid ointment. Now every once in a while, you'll hear the ambo called the zambuck.

The grey ghosts lurk beneath occupational captions taking their cue from clothing. The parking violations cops wear grey uniforms and come and go like ghosts before you can catch them.

Spruiker heads an unfamiliar column in the want

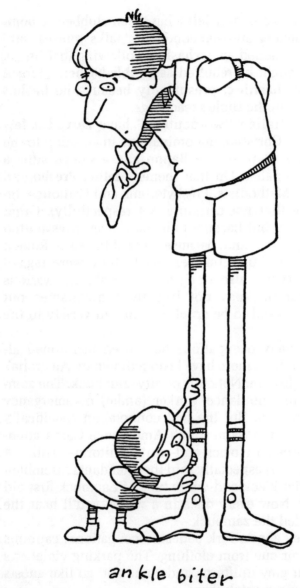

ankle biter

ads. Just as a hawker does, the department store **spruiker** stands in various departments announcing spot sales. The boisterous spruiker and the frenzied shoppers create pandemonium. A good spruiker draws crowds to his area like firefighters to an alarm.

Even some professions differ between speakers of English. You'll hear very little reference if any to lawyers or attorneys in Australia. When you have a legal dilemma, like trouble with a contract, you consult a **solicitor.** If you must take your case to a higher court, you'll be represented by a **barrister.** Australia, as other Commonwealth countries once under English rule, follows the British judicial system right down to the wearing of wigs, ruffles and gowns in the court. The barrister's clerk ("clark") or secretary, or anyone's secretary for that matter, wears the moniker **shiny bottom** because he sits all day long.

To fill a prescription you'll need a **chemist,** not a pharmacist—so do not look for a pharmacy on the corner. You'll find the **chemist** instead. A surgeon is called **mister,** not doctor; and nurses are **sisters.**

A **compere** hosts a television show or a stage event, just as an emcee does in the U.S. Emcee, of course, is an American bastardized construction, extracted from the initials M.C., the acronym for master of ceremonies. The TV news anchorman or anchorwoman is the **news presenter** of the **bulletin**—which is what Australians call the newscast.

No Antipodean colloquial list in any category would be complete without a group of clipped words. An airline stewardess has been retitled **hostess** which is always trimmed to **hostie.** Here are some others: **brickie,** a bricklayer; **deckie,** a deckhand on a boat; **flaggie,** a flagman at a road construction site. A **derro** is a derelict on the street (not unlike *wino*) and a **reffo** is a refugee. Again these terms on first hearing may not sound flattering, but they are not meant to be degrading either. Write it off to being a part of the relaxed Australian way of life, nothing more, nothing less.

The Aussie Battler

Another whole class of people in Australia are the **Aussie battlers.** They are not a club or an organization. The term befits the everyday Australian. It's their own phrase. An **Aussie battler** is the average Australian working person who's always trying to get ahead, to get more out of life, to get more from his salary, but never quite gets out from behind the eight ball. He keeps battling anyway. The battler means a great deal to Australians—probably from their colonial roots—men fighting a system that was harder, tougher and crueler than they were; men fighting nature which was stronger and fiercer than they. Today the Aussie battler is the working man, who has a bit less than what he wants.

In colloquial speech, the battler can label people with all sorts of strife. A person fighting a physical handicap is a battler; the widow left with several children is a battler; the old man trying to get through the day is a battler. People who hang the moniker on someone else, say it with pride in their commitment, courage and persistence. "A real **battler,** that one!" they will say as they take their hats off to him.

CHAPTER FOUR

Coo-ee!
That's Australian!

Early white settlers in Australia were a combination of free men and women and convicts or **transportees**— those transported by England to serve a prison sentence in the penal colony, starting in 1788 after the American Revolution. Together they were the equivalents of America's pioneers. They became master word-crafts-men, developing words adopted out of their forced isolation. The new vocabulary combined Anglicized aboriginal words, the melding of Scotch, Irish, Welsh, Cockney and other English dialects with new words born out of necessity. After all, necessity is the mother of invention in the mechanical world as well as the world of language.

The cry **"coo-ee!"** was once used to catch another's attention while walking through the wild where you could not be seen but might be heard. **"Coo-ee"** originates with the aboriginals who probably mimicked a bush bird's call. Since then, modern phrases have developed. "I can't believe I missed you at the mall Saturday. You must have been **within coo-ee."** (within the sound of my voice). But if you are **not within coo-ee,** you're a long way off. At a track meet, a disappointed coach might say: "My team wasn't **within coo-ee** of the finish." Also, **"Coo-ee!"** can be an exclamation, substituting for "Wow!"

Back of Beyond

"The Boondocks" or "the boonies" are two ways of describing faraway isolated places in American-English. While Aussies understand those terms they have a long list of names for remote locations not understood by most Americans, and they sound just as silly as "the boonies."

The **boo-ay** or **up the boo-ay** (pronounced "boo-EH") describes any outlying district. Today **the never-never** puts you in a similar spot, although originally **The Never-Never Land** referred to Northern Queensland and the Northern Territory of Australia only. They would be considered the farthest reaches of stock land where cattle grazed. That meaning perished. Now, when you **wander the never-never,** you're on **the wallaby track** or off to **woop woop,** in each case heading "God-knows-where."

You can ask for credit on **the never-never plan** and pay it off forever, with interest, of course. In modern terms, any use of a credit card might be called **the never-never plan.** The phrase is a holdover from the British, though it sounds more Australian these days.

Back of beyond and **back of Bourke** list as two more synonyms for somewhere in the **outback. Bourke** is the last New South Wales town on the edge of the great desert that fills the center of the Australian continent. A horserider would say of his mate, "He's been gone for a long time, probably **back of beyond** by now." Meanwhile, he could have ridden **beyond the black stump,** a legendary spot, and wind up in the same place that going **back of Bourke** took him, anywhere in the boonies.

Some towns in Australia claim to be home of the original **black stump** of legend—the charred remnants of a tree—but no town father has ever proved the phrase pointed to a real and not imaginary place.

Falling behind in anything—whether by distance or time—puts you **farther behind than Walla Walla,** another point on that fine undrawn line that divides civilization from the outback. Once a person is lost, he may find himself in the **backblocks,** away from the main street or on the outskirts of town. **Backblocks** translates into back streets also.

Walkabout means what it sounds like—to go walking about or **go for a wander.** But **walkabout** is connected directly with the aborigines. Something in the heritage of the aboriginals draws them back to their traditional homeland from time to time during their lives. The call may come at any time, no matter what other commitments the person might have. It's believed they return to their ancestral land for a kind of spiritual replenishment. The white settlers found **"walkabout"** a difficult concept to accept, especially if an aborigine worked for them as a drover or farm hand.

While the serious meaning of **walkabout** stands, the word has other connotations now. Anyone can go **walkabout,** whether to take a break for a few hours or take time off from work for a few days. Other common usage incudes "going for a walk." Picture the scenario: Dinner is over and an antsy son-in-law suggests going **walkabout.** He just wants to get some fresh air.

Billy and Blue

Billy represents much more than a boy's name in Oz. Mainly, **billy** equals a pot in which water is boiled over a campfire, usually for tea (a camp pot). A **Swaggie** always carries a billy or a **billycan.** The **billycan** may have started out as an old coffee tin. **Billy tongs** pick the hot pot off the campfire and pour the **billytea.** In these usages, **billy** derives its name from the aborigines' word *billa*, meaning water. An overflowing river or creek creates a **billabong** or a small runoff pond along its bank, a perfect calm spot to set up camp. A **jack shay** was another tin quart pot used like a billy to boil water or cook food.

A man who works like **billyo (billyoh)** does his job with gusto; if he **rides like billyo,** he rides as fast as the wind. But a horse that **goes off to billyo** loses his way or veers off the road. In which case, he may be on the **wallaby track!** If you **sit up like Jacky,** you stand with great pride—almost larger than life.

Willy, like his partner Billy, has not been left out. A **willy-willy** is a wind funnel filled with dust or sand which dances across a dry paddock, a dusty street or along a beach.

Blue stands on line behind his mates Willy and Billy to fill a lot of gaps in the Aussie nomenclature. They nickname redheaded boys **Blue** or **Bluey,** instead of naming them "Red," a play on words at the redhead's expense. Remember, we said **bluey** is the swagman's blue wool bedroll too. To **make a blue** means to make a mistake; and the guy who **cops the blue** takes the blame for it. Too much **turps** leaves a man **blue** (drunk) and that could bring on a **blue** in the pub (a fight or a brawl).

In addition to a blue, a **punch-up** may be a **stoush,** a **box-on,** a **barney** or a **boil-up.** A **boil-up** takes place when anger boils over. The **barney** could be brought on by an argument or an **argy-bargy** (argumentative) bloke. He's the kind of guy that gets **toey** (jumpy) in a crowd. At this point, the pub owner turns **ropeable** (fit to be tied) and his **cheese and kisses** (Mrs.) grows **aggro** (aggravated) with the lot of them. You can also have a **blue** at home, which would only be an argument rather than a punch-up.

Fair Go

To do anything fairly or give someone a fair chance is to offer a **fair go.** Labor unions use "Fair Go" as a banner and cry in the workplace. **Fair dinkum** has a similar background. Once it meant, literally, "honest work." Now, it stands for "honestly." A mother may ask her child if he's telling the truth and the boy could reply, **"Fair dinks,** Mum." Or "Honest, Mom." The most commonplace use of "fair dinkum" is when someone tells a tall story, and the listener asks in disbelief: "Fair dinkum?" The reply might be, "Dinkum, Mate."

Add one more term for work or manual labor. **Yakker** comes dressed in brown overalls or navy blue laborers' shorts, covered with sweat. "Building that fence in the hot sun was **hard yakker!**" Or a farmer who bought a plot of bad land has a **hard yakker** ahead of him.

Sticky Beak and a Bibful

When an event heats up in America, it **hots up** Down Under. Heating up and **hotting up** are twins. When something exciting or out of the ordinary happens, out come the **sticky beaks** hand-in-hand with the "nosey bodies." **Sticky beaks** stick their noses or beaks into other people's business. A sticky beak can **take a sticky**

beak too, by "nosing around" or browsing. Sometimes the whole phrase will be shortened to **having a sticky** or **taking a sticky.** If you go to visit a friend's new home for the first time, you may ask to **have a sticky,** a look around. But a **sticky beak** may also be a snoop—putting the nose in where it's not supposed to be. If you just want a quick look at something, you'll **squiz.**

When you relate embarrassing or off-color stories you **split a bibful.** The receiver winds up with **a bibful** when you're done telling tales. The **bibful** of gossip may be out and out lies. On the other hand, it could be **spot on** or **bang on** the truth; in which case, the teller "hit the nail on the head." But if it's all in fun and everyone is just teasing, they are **taking the mickey out of you!** Aussies absolutely love to **take the mickey out** of someone at any given time!

Just Beaut!

"Your new car is **just beaut!**" It's terrific, wonderful, great! **Beaut** can describe anything but it is always a compliment; unlike "beaut" in American slang which more than likely is sarcastic and negative. In the U.S. you might call a rude person "a beaut."

Bonzer! and **Grouse!** double as **beaut's** best Aussie mates. **Grouse** has been adopted as an Aussie teen-age term, something a Down Under "Val-gal" might say. If something is beyond terrific, beyond wonderful, call it **ripper!** A great buy is a **ripper.** A fan at a **footy** match may shout **"ripper!"** at the end of a big play.

In search of another compliment to serve, try **"good on ya!"**—a way of saying, "You've done well. We're proud of you."

When I get **tinny** (very lucky) I'm **rapt** about it. **Rapt,** meaning thrilled or excited, probably comes from "in rapture." Someone else will be **happy as Larry** when life goes his way. Some oral tradition says the **Larry** in the phrase stems from the word **larrikan** which originally meant a fool. But **Larry** has moved away from that definition and now he's the happiest man in the world.

The same bloke will tell you **"Everything's apples!"** or **"She's apples!"** Just as likely, he'll exclaim, **"She's sweet!"** **"She,"** in this context, replaces "everything" as in the idiom **"She'll be right, mate."** The translation is "Things will get better," or to use another Aussie expression, "It'll **come good."**

To **come good** can move in similar circles in relation to people. If a guy owes you money but you believe he'll repay you, you would comment, "He'll come good." Similarly, a kid who has been notoriously bad all along might "come good in the end" by changing his ways and going straight.

To Come a Cropper

Another myriad of phrases describes times "when things go bad." A deal turns sour and the bloke making the deal **comes a cropper.** "Fred's business was doing so well, then it **came a cropper** (hit the skids)." Fred may try for a desperate comeback by betting on **Sydney or the bush,** which means he's going for all or nothing and he may wind up with a **basinful of trouble.**

With a **basinful** like that, Fred does not have "a chance in Hell" of turning things around and that measures up to having **Buckley's chance.** Poor **Buckley** had no chance at all. The etymology of Buckley's chance has blurred badly with time. Some say it stems from William Buckley, an early escaped convict who lived among aborigines with no chance of ever returning to Great Britain. (By the way, this William Buckley would have been an es-ca-PEE, not an es-CAPE-ee.)

An independent man might live by **Rafferty's rules,** meaning no rules at all—another blurry etymology here. Like **Buckley, Rafferty** may have begun as a slight aimed at Irish immigrants, since both are Irish surnames adopted as colloquial speech. No matter how the phrases began, it is clear now that when you live by **Rafferty's rules,** you will have **Buckley's chance** of escaping the law! In New Zealand, where the language takes another twist, **rafferty** with a small r equals rough or ragged.

When a person is confused and doesn't know whether he's coming or going, the Aussies say he doesn't know **if he's Arthur or Martha!** But, if he knows exactly where he's heading and he is seeking adventure, he's probably **as game as Ned Kelly.** That's ready and willing to undertake anything put before him, just like the **bushranger** Ned Kelly did in his legendary lifetime. Over the years, Kelly and his gang covered more than a few miles **on the frog and toad** (rhyming slang for road) running from the police.

Flog the Cat!

A colorful image **to flog the cat** unfortunately sounds similar to "beating a dead horse." But **don't flog the cat** does not mean "Don't repeat yourself." It's more specific than that. It commands you not to complain over and over about the same thing. While we're at it, whining and complaining equal **whinging** and the whiner gets labeled a **whinger.** Mum scolds the whining child, "Don't **whinge!**" And a co-worker fed up with someone's constant complaining will refer to the person as **a real whinger.**

A person who has nothing to whinge about and has become outstanding in his or her field falls into the **tall poppy** category. A **tall poppy** is an achiever who becomes well known in the process—a notable. Most tall poppies gain their status through positive means in government positions or industry. Others might be entertainers or communicators, doctors or research scientists.

Most people work very hard to become tall poppies, some possibly to the point of exhaustion. At the end of each day, they're **all in** or **buggered.** When they're *that* tired, they may **bugger** something **up** by making a mistake (or a **blue**). But to try and fail beats doing **bugger all**—which means doing nothing whatsoever. The **bludger** whom we've met before goes through life doing **bugger all!**

Bullswool!

"Ah, baloney!" translates into **"bollocks!"** or **"bullo!"** or **"that's bullswool!"** All of them fall into a heap of rubbish! **All that bizzo** adds up to a lot of nonsense, too.

But, if you are standing in the **bullocky** or you are simply **bols** it would be quite a shock to find you running down a street. You would be dressed only in your birthday suit! Someone might scream, **"Hoolydooly!** He's **starkers!"** **Starkers** comes from stark naked and **hooly-dooly** expresses surprise, much like "Holy Cow!" It's an old-fashioned phrase seldom heard these days.

A sarcastic phrase that no one seems to know the history of is **"How's your father?"** or more true to sound: **" 'ow's yer father?"** This is not a polite question or greeting. Instead it's an adjectival phrase that degrades whatever it is used to modify. An example may clarify this strange one. If you ate in a restaurant where the food was bad and service worse, you would tell your friends afterwards: "I wouldn't eat there again. It

was a bit **'ow's yer father!"** Not up to standard, lousy. Strange? Maybe. True? Fair dinkum.

In most cases, this book does not discuss curse words or the slang of the street, but I will offer two words here that may save some unknowing Yanks from embarrassment.

After a sumptuous meal where you've consumed everything in sight you may feel stuffed. Fair enough! But, if an Aussie tells you, **"Get stuffed!"** he's not talking about eating. **Stuffed,** here, has the same foul connotation as the four-letter word which you could imagine in its place. Not polite at all.

The word **root** can fill the same blank. So you don't "root for a team" in Oz. That would make you a bit more intimate than a cheerleader. Instead, you **barrack** for a team. **Barrack** has an aboriginal history—first meaning to jeer at your enemy. Then it became synonymous with cheering for a side. In modern times, especially when it comes to **footy,** you **barrack for** your favorite team and **barrack against** its opponents. If you do slip up, **no worries!** (Don't worry). The Aussies will just **take the Mickey** out of you for a little while.

A ballplayer with butterfingers may feel **dicky** that day (unsteady) particularly if **aunty** broadcasts the game. **Aunty** stands for the ABC or **Australian Broadcasting Company,** an equivalent of England's BBC. This government-funded television and radio network reaches all of Australia's cities and towns, including those **up the boo-ay** to where commercial stations could never afford to transmit. The ABC earned the pseudonym **aunty** from critics for "being as stuffy as my old aunt!"

Corroboree

Just as **barrack** and **billabong** do, other aboriginal-based words slither softly through the language of the

Antipodes. A **corroboree** is a celebration, a festival. The music of an aboriginal corroboree comes from the **didgeridoo** (pronounced did-jer-ree-DO), a primitive woodwind instrument that releases an eerie sort of melody.

A **dillybag** serves as a small carrier sack and a **humpy** describes a crude mud brick dwelling.

Station Life

Along the way, we've met the **swaggies,** the **cockies** and the **jackeroos**—the real-life characters from Australia's bush, but we haven't been introduced to some of the phrases turned by Aussie station dwellers.

Remember it's here where the **cocky,** the **grazier** and the **pastoralist** remain king. (More in Chapter Two). The **squatter** is also a landowner. It stems from the early years of Australia. The closest thing to a squatter in America was a homesteader.

Picture the Australia of Colleen McCullough's *The Thornbirds*—a vast cattle **station** (ranch) which never seems to end. The **home paddock** surrounds the main house. A **paddock** in Oz does not connote only a turf field for grazing. Instead, any field is a paddock, whether corn shoots up from the ground as straight as toy soldiers or whether cows graze lazily on golden hay. The **back paddock** compares to the "North 40," the section of the property farthest away from the house.

Barns do not stand in the farmyards of most of Australia (with the exception of a few areas settled by Germans). Most farm buildings fall under the heading **shed.** Every outbuilding, expansive or tiny, is a **shed.**

Station owners construct most sheds out of corrugated tin and aluminum—the walls as well as the roof. Many have only three sides. All of them lack the style of a big sturdy American barn. (One thing's for sure, no one will ever refurbish a shed in a hundred years and turn it into a house. By then it will probably rust.)

The **chooks** live in a shed, albeit a little one. A **chook?** A **chook** is a chicken, a hen old enough to lay eggs or be roasted for Sunday dinner. A little **chook** is actually called a **chicken.** Don't worry, they've left the rooster alone.

On the cattle station, young bull calves sold for veal can be called **mickey calves** or **bobby calves.** A **mickey** is usually the wildest calf in the bunch. The **poddy calf** may live among the mickeys and the bobbies, too. It is the orphan which must be fed by hand. You raise a **poddy lamb** the same way.

Most farms have man-made ponds somewhere on the grounds, sometimes for the animals, sometimes for irrigation. Australian farms have them, too, but they do not call them ponds or waterholes. They are **dams.** It's strange to hear that cows drink *from* dams and children swim *in* **dams,** but Down Under they do. In the hot summer, kids may also dive into a **bogie,** another word for swimming hole.

With nothing better to do, the youngsters may lie back and count all the clouds in the **apple pie!** What? Remember the rules for rhyming slang. **Pie** rhymes with sky. That solves it.

Driveway is too fancy a word as far as Aussie cockies are concerned. They prefer to call their driveways **tracks. Tracks** can be any unpaved road surface throughout a property, like the track to the shearing shed or the back paddock. Paved surfaces are referred to as **bitumen.** That's "bitch-u-men," their version of blacktop or asphalt.

On a sheep station, the shearers in the **shearing shed** or **wool shed** have a language all their own. Here are a few examples: The **broomie** sweeps up the floor and separates the **dags** from the wool. **Dags** are the sheep "dirt" (a familiar euphemism, I trust) and other "crud" caught in the fleece around the animals' "bottom." I mention these unpleasantries because the word **dag** has been carried off the station and gladly transported to the cities. A **dag** now denotes an outcast, someone unsociable or untrendy, who "dresses **daggy**" or "wears **daggy** clothes." He may be classified as "such a **dag**!"— a stigma shunned by all.

A young shearer aspires to be **the ringer,** the top shearer in the shed—it's most likely the source of our colloquial term "ringer." In sports, Americans call an athlete a ringer when he or she outplays everyone else—like a pro put into amateur competition or a collegiate player up against teen-agers. The **board-boy** stands alongside the broomie as another wool shedhand.

When the shearers and the boys are ready for a break, they take a **smoko.** A **smoko** originally meant stopping for a smoke, but then the definition widened to mean a break—a cigarette and/or a cup of tea or coffee and a snack, any kind of break from a hard day. Even a brochure for a riding school advertises "Full afternoon bush rides (smoko included) for experienced riders only." The **smoko** in that case means they'll stop and supply tea and a biscuit midway through the ride.

Aussie slang for a cigarette has been stolen from the British. Instead of a "butt," someone will ask for a **fag.** Remember, fag does not carry the American slang connotation.

On a weekend, the shearers, broomies and folks from the surrounding district may get invitations to a **woolshed hop,** just an old-fashioned barn dance or hoedown.

One of the trained sheep dogs is the **backing dog.** He brings up the rear of the flock or **the mob.** While **mob** means flock in this case, any group of people or things in Oz gets dubbed a **mob.**

Perhaps the worst parts of station life are the **blowies** and the **mozzies.** They create tandem trouble. **Blowies,** short for blowflies, are flies, and **mozzies** are mosquitoes. Whatever they're called, they still buzz and sting the same. There just seem to be more of them in Australia.

Together the blowies and the mozzies gave birth to an important piece of Australiana—**the Aussie salute. Salute** befits the act of swatting flies away from the face, a constant activity in the bush. Hardcore **swagmen** and **bushies** wore corks dangling from their hat brims to keep the blowies away.

The **cockies** come to town for **The Royal Show.** The **show** compares with American state fairs. Primarily an agricultural show, city families flock to it as well to see the prize bulls, the baking contests, crafts displays, lumberjacks and you-name-it. Each region has an annual show where kids scurry to get their **showbags.** They began as sample giveaways, full of surprises, but now they're filled with everything from snackfood to Barbie™ doll supplies and are sold virtually for the price of the contents. While the kids rush to buy them, Mum ends up carrying an armful of colorful showbags. It's quite a sight!

Almost a Royal

While we've established that **bickies** are crackers and cookies Down Under, we haven't looked at their other place in the colloquial lexicon. Bickies are "bucks," "dough," money. Something that costs "big bucks" can just as easily cost **big bickies!**

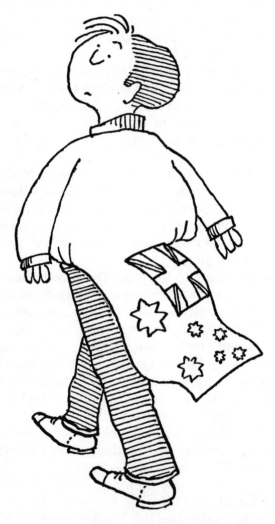

the Australian flag

The Aussie monetary system has been based on the Australian dollar since the 1960s. Before that it followed the British system. The Australian prime minister during the changeover didn't want to call his decimal system "the dollar" and requested "the royal" instead. I'm sure many people mused: "The royal what?" and voted against it.

Twenty-five-cent pieces do not exist in Australia, hence there are no quarters. The 20-cent piece is the common denomination used in pay phones and vending machines. The one-dollar note died in 1984 and successfully gave way to one-dollar coins. The two-dollar note has outlived its smaller cousin, but has been followed by a two-dollar coin as well.

The Australian vocabulary is unfamiliar with "nickels" and "dimes" and all the colloquialisms which have grown up around them in America. "Five-and-dime stores" and "the five and ten" do not relate to anything. Woolworth's is not even a five-and-ten down there. It is a supermarket and a well-known one. When you think about it, the original basis of such a name, stores with goods costing only five and ten cents, has been long gone in the U.S., too. Now, if you thought a chain store like Woolworth's slipped through the fingers of the word clippers, you are wrong. They fondly call Woolworth's **Woolies.**

Since there are no nickels and dimes, no one "stops on a dime" or "turns on a dime." They "can't earn a dime" or "rub two nickels together" either. No one thinks in terms of a "plug nickel" or "nickling and diming someone" into bankruptcy.

Oddly, the Australians have one-cent and two-cent pieces, but *penny* does not live in their lexicon. Hence, no child can be "as bright as a penny." To fill the void created by the absence of pennies, nickels and dimes,

two-bob watch

the Aussies hold onto the British words for coins, **bob** and **quid**. A **bob** was a shilling and a **quid** was a pound. Someday, they will be obsolete as the use of the English monetary system (or the "old money," as they sometimes call it) falls farther into history; but, until then, phrases like: "He's as **crazy as a two-bob watch**" and "Loan me a quid" remain very much a part of Down Under's spoken language.

What's a **two-bob watch**? It's a cheap one that doesn't work very well and can never get the time right!

Hellos and Good-bye

Everyone knows Aussies say, **"G'day!"** That's the contraction for "Good Day" but they not only contract the spelling but the sound as well. The "Good" is just a quick "G" sound rolled off the tongue and squashed against the "Day." It has become their universal greeting, unique among English-speaking people.

For good-bye, you will hear other phrases which sound a bit British. **"Cheers!"** is one. Of course, "Cheers!" may also be a toast with a drink in hand. But, if someone says it walking out the door, you know they mean, "So long, farewell."

In addition to cheers, **hooroo** shows up. It's another old-fashioned salutation that you hear from time to time instead of "see you later."

So, "Hooroo, see you in the next chapter."

CHAPTER FIVE

Queuing Up with Everyday Words

Just as everyone eats, everyone wears clothes. Clothing is not much different in Australia from that worn in the United States; there are no traditional costumes like the ones found in Europe, except those brought in by immigrants from different lands. No gay folk dresses or headpieces designed to change with every jig, reel or *tarantella*. But, even though our clothes are much the same, they hide behind skirts of different names and that may cause some confusion.

On a cool afternoon Down Under we have a choice of **jumpers, cardies, sloppy joes** or **windcheaters** to fight the chill. An interesting set of choices! The first two are sweaters and the second pair substitutes for sweatshirts. But what job in the wardrobe do each of these perform? You may be surprised.

Women wear **jumpers** and so do men! There's nothing strange about a man or a boy in a **jumper** because jumper fills the same gap in the dresser drawer as a pullover of any kind. It could be a **rugby** or **footy jumper.** Then again, it may be a fine hand-knitted jumper made of the best **merino** wool or a workman's jumper created from **greasy wool. Greasy** doesn't mean dirty. It's the Aussie term for the kind of wool that still has lanolin in it, used in many countries particularly for sailing sweaters and hats because the natural oil keeps water from seeping into the knit.

Obviously, this **jumper** would never get confused with the woman's sleeveless dress worn over a blouse. Women do wear similar frocks in Oz but they call them **pinafores** or **pinnies.** In my mind, a pinafore conjures up pictures of frilly apron-fronted dresses worn by little girls on holidays. It strikes me as strange to talk about adults wearing pinafores.

Pinnies are another story. If you've ever played intramural school sports you may remember the term "pinnies." They are the short colored squares tied around your top so players can tell which player belongs to which team. So while American pinnies and Australian pinnies are not the same, the word appears in both countries. We will find a number of clothing homonyms that have distinct meanings.

Polo jumpers refer to turtleneck sweaters, with **polo collar** standing in for turtleneck. *Polos* never mean the summery knit shirts Americans wear. They're just collared sport shirts. The Aussie word-clippers use **cardie** as an excuse for cardigan. No real mystery there! But it is quite cute to hear an elderly couple remind each other to bring a **cardie** along.

While sloppy joes in the U.S.A. are those saucy hamburger meat sandwiches, the Aussies have chosen to call sweatshirts that instead. I suppose someone in a fleecy **jumper** was told once he looked like a "Sloppy Joe" and the name stuck! A **windcheater** makes more sense. You put a pullover on "to cheat the wind"—but Americans might choose a windbreaker over a sweatshirt for the same purpose.

On a very cold day, Australians will be happy to put on a **skivvy** to go outside! Crazy? Not really. A **skivvy** is a cotton long-sleeved turtleneck, not underclothes.

You may think you know what **knickers** are when people talk about them. But, be careful! They are not what you may suppose. Knickers are ladies' underpants. It probably stems from a time when undergarments were knee length, like bloomers. Today, knickers mean even the tiniest, laciest briefs.

In this land of sun and fun, jumpers number among the heaviest clothes worn in much of the country and swimsuits may be considered the most traditional Australian costume in modern times. In different regions, swimmers' wear varies by name. They could be **bathers, togs** or **cozzies** (what little there are of any of them). The odd one in the bunch, **cozzie,** takes its name from the clipped version of **bathing costume.** Get it?

Along with togs, Aussies slip on a pair of **sandshoes** that bear an uncanny resemblance to sneakers.

Men who work outdoors have their own unofficial uniform for workday dress. It consists of navy blue short shorts known as **stubbies,** after a brand name, and navy blue singlets made of cotton or wool. Woolen sleeveless shirts, often worn by farmers or sheepshearers, have taken the nickname **Jacky Howe,** after a champion sheepshearer of the 1890s.

Country Clothes/City Fashions
On the farm or station, a few other "musts" exist. **Gumbies** block the back doorway of the house when not covering feet to save them from the mud or dung.

Gumbies or **gumboots** describe any kind of rubber boots, also known as **wellingtons** or **wellies**—the last two terms handed down by the British.

The signs of a grazier are his **Driz-a-Bone** and **Akubra**. The **Driz-a-Bone** trademark is derived from the simile "dry as a bone" and it befits the heavy brown oiled-cotton overcoat worn by stockmen and farmers. The cotton breathes in the heat and cold, and the oil creates the same effect as oil in a duck's feathers. Water rolls right off.

The Akubra brand name tags many of the stockman's hats worn throughout the bush country. At first glance they resemble American cowboy hats but a keen eye can spot variations in styles between the American West and the Australian bush headwear. Other hat-makers create bush headgear but Akubra is certainly the best known.

Another classic is the **R.M.Williams** boot. It is ankle high and has a narrow top with thick elastic insets to keep it tight fitting on the leg. The tightness at the ankle deters the creepy-crawlies from slithering out of the bush and sneaking inside the shoe and getting to the feet. When someone wants to keep the creatures from going the other direction, up the pants leg, they tie **bowyangs** around the fabric. **Bowyangs** are usually leather shoestrings, but any string or fabric can do the job.

Moleskins share the same closet with the rest of the bushgear. These traditional buff-colored pants follow the style of Western jeans but, instead of denim, they are made of a soft brushed cotton fabric called moleskin. Like Western clothing in the U.S., bush clothes underwent a revival in Australia, making boots, hats and moleskins trendy for city wear as well as country gear. Breaking with tradition, moleskins come in a selection of colors and a variety of price tags to boot! It depends on whether the shop is located in Toorak or Korumburra. That's the difference between trendy Fifth Avenue and Waco, Texas.

School Days

Australian children either attend **state schools** or **public schools.** That sounds like the same thing, but it is not. **State schools** equal our public schools; state-run, meaning publicly-funded schools. **Public schools** are just the opposite of what they sound like. They are the private schools, equivalent to the British preparatory schools.

The first year in school is **kindie,** short for kindergarten. (*Kindergarten,* you may want to note, is adopted from the German. The direct translation is "children's garden.") A **college** is very often a high school or secondary school but it can be attached to the name of any private school. It is not the equivalent of *university.* Therefore, if an Australian begins a story, "When I was at college . . . ," he is probably talking about his teen years.

Children wear uniforms to both state and public schools. They are similar to the uniforms worn in American parochial schools. Little girls don **pinnies;** older girls, wool skirts and blazers in winter; and both age groups have lightweight dresses for the summer months. Boys usually wear grey flannel trousers and blazers. But uniform shorts enter the summer-time picture, especially for the **littlies** (make that "little ones").

Shorts and summer frocks are important in Oz because the days can get very hot. The kids do not get three months summer vacation. Instead, they get a six-week **holiday** (vacation) during the Christmas period (which remember is the height of summer) and a cou-

aussie schoolboy

ple of weeks here and there during the rest of the calendar year. Each school year begins in January, after the Christmas break.

Older girls may bring **handbags** to school but no girl or woman in Australia ever carries a "pocketbook." According to them, a pocketbook is strictly American. Children living in Queensland tote their schoolbooks to and from school in a **port.** That is the shortened version of *portmanteau*, a word used by the British to mean suitcase, obviously borrowed from the French. **Port** generally means any small carrying case or book-bag in Queensland, but nowhere else in the country.

In addition to most of the paraphernalia kids carry to and from school, Aussie kids take **rubbers** along too. No, it's not that rainy. They don't bring galoshes with them everywhere, just **rubbers. Rubbers** are rubber pencil erasers, nothing else.

Hats comprise an important part of the school uniform. Wool felt **tit-fors** (remember tit-for-tat rhymes with hat) partner with the winter clothes and old-fashioned straw boaters and girls' bonnets with long ribbons down the back are part of the summer dress code.

Little girls may have **fringe** under their hats and long **plats** (or **plaits**) down the sides. **Plats** and **fringe** have nothing to do with the hats; they are a part of the girl's hairstyle. **Fringe** substitutes for bangs and **plats** are braids. Instead of braiding hair, Mum **plats** her daughter's hair.

An unkempt little **digger** may add an **Australian flag** to his uniform. Some say it's the official dresswear of Oz. It means the little guy's shirttail is hanging out the back of his pants and waving about like a flag!

Mum or dad may give children an allowance to pay for school items, and they might say, "Put it **in your**

kick." The **kick** fills the same gap as "kitty," a place to put your money.

Around the House and Garden

The rooms, furniture and parts of an Australian house have many labels which differ from those used in America. Even the living room has not been spared. Families sit in their **lounge rooms,** as if they were a public waiting room. They purchase **lounge suites** (matching sofa, chairs, etc.) to fill the **lounge.**

While visiting a private home, you may need to avail yourself of a toilet. Things are changing, but this simple task may be a bit more complex than you would imagine. The **toilet** is just that, a little room with a toilet in it, sometimes accompanied by a sink, but not necessarily! Sometimes Australians refer to the **loo,** which is a carry over from the British. If you really want to freshen up, you inquire about the bathroom. But, keep in mind, the bathroom may not have a toilet in it!

The fine line drawn between **toilet** and **bathroom** and the existence of sinkless toilets and toilet-less bathrooms stems from the late 1950s and early 60s when **the dunny** finally gave way to sewage. The dunny sits comfortably alongside the outhouse in history but outlived the American ones by decades. In suburban backyards **dunnies** stood in the **garden** (yard), however small, for family use. Beneath the seat was a huge can or metal drum which collected the refuse and was picked up and replaced monthly by the **dunnyman** on the **dunny truck.** (We won't speculate what this was like in the heat of an Aussie summer with the **blowies,** flies, going wild!)

With sewers installed (thank goodness!), toilets became the "in thing;" but few middleclass homeowners rearranged their baths to accommodate the toilet; instead, they gave it a room of its own.

In modern homes, a full bath adjoining a bedroom takes on a fancy French phrase, en suite. **En suite** in Australia has come to mean only the bedroom/ bathroom arrangement. Nothing else.

In the kitchen, a number of differences catch the cook's eye. Cookbooks must be translated like foreign novels for the American recipe reader. To begin with, Australia follows the metric system, which means a cup measures more than a U.S. cup, though it sounds the same. All measures need to be converted.

Recipes call for **corn flour** instead of corn starch. You won't find baking soda either, only bicarbonate of soda. Both red or green peppers are **capsicums.**

Like "veggies" in the U.S., vegetables have taken on pet names: **mushies, 'nanas** and **avos** (mushrooms, bananas and avocados) to name a few.

Broiled meat and fish cook in a **griller** and come out **grilled.** I suppose grilled cheese does, too.

The **electric jug** or **electric kettle** replaced the **billy** indoors in Australia. The electric pot may be a **birko** also, a tradename now in common use around the house. All of them make a quick **cuppa** (cup of tea or coffee) and that's important!

You set the table with **serviettes,** another word from the French, not napkins. **Napkins** have another job and it has to do with baby. Look for napkins or **nappies** where you would find diapers, maybe next to the **cot.** While **cot** always denotes a crib, it may refer to any size bed, depending on the context. "Jumping in the cot" means jumping in the sack or hitting the hay. A man may be surprised to learn he can **nurse** a baby Down Under. Anyone cuddling or holding a little one **nurses** the child. In this way, nursing is not automatically synonymous with breast-feeding.

When Australians need bed sheets and towels for their homes they shop for **manchester.** The **manchester department** carries all household linens. The name reflects history. Manchester, England, was a textile town. Bedding shoppers do not bother looking for "January white sales" because linens do not count as white goods. **White goods** denote big-ticket appliances such as washers, dryers, refrigerators, etc., which used to be all white. Remember those days?

When stores hold their after-Christmas sales, the **queues** grow impossible to deal with. **Queuing up** is an art similar to standing in line (or on line, depending on where you live in the U.S.), but often there is no true line to stand on. The **queue** resembles a mob with each person taking his or her turn at **fronting the till** or standing in front of the cash register. A shopper needing a lay away plan will put his goods on **lay-by.**

Myer, one of Australia's largest and oldest department stores, is as well known as Macy's in New York and Harrod's in London. When someone puts on airs he **wears a front as big as Myer,** meaning his actions are all a big facade!

A woman who shows off her newly purchased clothes, promenading up and down the main streets in town, is said to be **doing the block.** The phrase can be used in lots of different ways to mean "showing off."

In a department store or any other building, including a **flat block** or a **block of flats** (apartment house or complex), the floor above the ground floor equals the **first floor.** So if you live in the middle of a three-story house, you reside in a **first-floor flat.**

Aussies never sit on a porch. They sit on **verandas.** To most Americans the veranda trims the sides of a big

ranch house, open and airy. A porch is a porch, roman-
tic, gracious and welcoming. But, in Australia, there is
no distinction. **Veranda** even refers to petit city porches
surrounded by flowers and rosebushes.

Someone may tell you they grew up on an **estate** in
Oz. Don't be impressed. They mean **housing estate,** the
equivalent of a housing development.

While the name **terrace houses** makes these inner
city dwellings sound grander than rowhouses or even
brownstones, they fit the same basic concept: one- or
two-story adjoining houses (rarely three stories in Oz).
The more stylish **terraces,** built during Victoria's reign,
are in demand these days, following the brownstone
revival in New York and variations on the theme
throughout the world. Special features in good and
once grand terrace houses are the wrought iron lace-
work on upper and lower balconies reminiscent of the
New Orleans French Quarter and **leadlight** windows
and doors. **Leadlight** is the term for any stained glass.

The bush tumbles into the language of the house just
as it does into most sectors of the Australian lexicon.
An old-fashioned household cure—something grand-
mother might hand down—is a **bush-cure.** A **bush-cure**
comes in handy when someone is **crook,** which means
they're sick. The neighborhood grapevine has nothing
over the **bush telegraph** when it comes to spreading
gossip, rumor or information.

Birko and **zambuck** have been mentioned as manufacturers' tradenames adopted by everyday speech
over the years. Three more run amok daily: **biro, texta**
and **wettex.** The biro relates to ballpoint pens; **texta** to a
kind of ink marker and **wettex** to a spongy cloth used
for household cleaning.

Clothes pegs secure laundry hung on the clothesline
or the **hoist,** not clothespins. The **Hill's hoist,** to be

specific, stands in almost every suburban garden. The contraption is similar to clothesline stands in America, which look a bit like bare beach umbrellas stuck in the ground. The beauty of a hoist is simple: It lowers to make it easier to hang clothes and raises up high so no one runs into it. On all counts, the hoist is ugly; but, like a television antenna on a roof, its practical use outweighs its appearance.

Aussie idioms exchanged between friends may throw off an unknowing outsider, probably more than they realize. To ask a friend to wait a minute you say, **"Just a tick,"** and when something will be done in a jiffy, it'll be **done in a tick!** But if you expect it a week from Friday, you can expect it **Friday week** (or **Monday week, Tuesday week,** etc.).

At morning teatime or late in the day when work is put aside, the men may indulge in a **smoko.** That's when they take a break from their chores to smoke a cigarette or have a **cuppa.** The cup after work may be filled with something other than tea to be sure!

Men throw a **buck's party** for their mate who's engaged to be married instead of a stag party or a bachelor's party. Not to be outdone, the women hold a **hen's party** for the "girls" only. Most of them are a little more lively than a bridal shower.

Outside the house the car plays an important role in Australian life, mainly because the country is so big and sprawling. The terms dealing with cars are very British. Aussies even drive on the left side of the road and fill their cars with **petrol,** not gasoline. The mechanic checks under the **bonnet** to make sure everything operates properly. The driver stows the spare **tyre** in the **boot** (trunk). A **ute** is a car without a boot! It has an open back, half car/half pick up, similar to an "El

Camino" but not as sporty. **Ute** substitutes for **utility wagon.**

A **combi** is a Volkswagen bus outfitted as a combination (combi) car and camper or **campervan.** Volkswagen is commonly shortened to **vee-dub;** even "V.W." is too many syllables for the Aussies. Another recreational vehicle is a **caravan,** the kind of camper-trailer which you tow by car and then set up on site at a **caravan park.**

Australians always make fun of the great big cars Americans drive, like Cadillacs and Lincolns. They call them **Yank tanks.** For all of that, if you have an old one in Australia, it has become a collector's item.

All of these vehicles and any other ones must be registered. When they talk about registration, Aussies talk about, you guessed it, the **reggo** (pronounced REGE-jo). And the plates on the car are the **reggo plates,** not license plates. License is spelled "licence," like "defence." At this point, what else would you expect from our Aussie mates?

A young man trying to push his new car to the limit will brag of **doing the ton** or hitting the 100-mile-per-hour mark. That's another phrase which may fall to the changeover in the metric system since distance is measured in kilometers now, not miles anymore.

The bloke who's **done the ton** and had a **prang** (an accident) in the process will need the help of a **panel beater** to put his car back in shape. The **panel beater** occupies a place in the auto body shop. He'll straighten out your **mudguards** (fenders) and anything else smashed in the **prang.**

Hiding in the toolbox will be a **spanner.** A workman reaches for a **spanner** instead of a wrench in Australia. Therefore, in colloquial speech if someone **mucks it up,** he's thrown a **spanner** in the works. Leave the wrench in the U.S.A.

On a lighter motoring note, a family may **go for a burl** or a leisurely drive on a Sunday afternoon. They'll pack up lunch and throw some **softdrinks** and ice in the **esky**. **Esky** commonly denotes an ice chest or cooler. It comes from the Esky brand name, like Thermos in the States. A **burl** makes for a pleasant afternoon, but then, Aussies do appreciate their free time and that makes it a lovely country to visit and tour.

CHAPTER SIX

The Games Aussies Play

The Aussies are great outdoors people. After all, they have the kind of space few other nations can claim—only 17 million people in a country the size of the continental United States. That grants them plenty of room to spread out and have a good time. And they do! Add the space to the amount of leisure time. The country is based on a 37-and-a-half-hour workweek, with at least six to eight paid holidays a year, plus five to six weeks paid vacation annually. In most cases unused vacation time can be stored up year to year if not used. How's that? (As the Aussies tend to ask.)

Since the majority of that small population lives within an hour's drive to the ocean, all ages enjoy all sorts of water sports. Yachting, swimming, surfing, wind surfing (or sailboarding) and water skiing number among the most popular.

Of course, if you know anything about Australians you know they are **mad keen** yachties, whether they actually sail or just watch. The final proof, in their eyes, of their strength was winning the America's Cup 12-metre races in Newport, Rhode Island, in 1983. They'd rather not talk about the loss on their home waters in 1987.

If yachting is your interest in Australia and you've skipped directly to this chapter hoping to be told enough about Australian-English to get you through a day on and off the waves with a crew from Down Under—sorry! You'll have to read Chapter One to find out what they say when they are not throwing around yachting jargon, and certainly you'll need to read Chapter Two to find out what you'll be eating and, most of all, drinking so you'll know how to enjoy the victory party. Someone may offer you a **stubby** or a **pony** or invite you to **hit the turps!** Then what? You may even find yourself at a **barby** with a few **prawns** or **bangers** on the grill. Whatever the case, enjoy the merrymaking with the other **septics** and **pommies** who might have gone along too. (You'll find out what they are later.)

So leave the nautical lingo to the race course (and the maritime dictionary) and concentrate on the social scene. Oh! Better check Chapter Three to find out who **sheila** is and when to call someone a **mate!**

Even if you're not planning to go to Oz, but you sail elsewhere, the rest of the Aussie language will come in handy dockside anywhere in the world, because if there's a boat, water and sunshine, there's bound to be an Aussie **boatie within coo-ee!**

Swimming is a major pastime and the miles of free open beaches that surround the island nation are watched closely by volunteer lifeguards who are members of local **surf livesaving clubs** or **S.L.C.s.**

The surf livesavers are the fellows and girls who wear colored swim caps and tank tops. They are proficient not only in swimming but also in surf-skis (a cross between surfboards and kayaks with paddles) and surf lifeboats, rowed by teams through the heavy ocean waves. To prove their athletic prowess, the S.L.C. teams compete during **surf carnivals** every year, giving them a competitive reason to remain in shape. They must run, swim, row and act out saving lives for points. It looks like a beachcombers' triathalon. The surf carnival is a fun time for the town that holds it and worth being a part of, even if you're just visiting. Everyone comes out to watch.

A water sport that created another subculture in Australia is surfing. The **surfies** or **boardies** live lives reminiscent of old Gidget movies and have a beach language unique to their lifestyle. Their jargon is not part of mainstream Australian-English except perhaps in beach communities. However, some words do sneak into common usage. **Boomers** are the big waves anywhere and surfies' **cozzies** and **board shorts** (they are long-legged surfers' swimsuits) accompanied by colorful singlets. They walk around with zinc cream on their noses to block the sun, and thongs (those rubber sandals) on their feet to keep their soles above the hot sand.

Those not game enough to take on surfing may take part in a more passive but time consuming leisure activity, sunbathing on a **lilo. Lilo?** It's a brandname for an inflatable vinyl raft. No Aussie ever talks about a raft, only a "Lie-low." Get it? They even take them camping as air matresses.

Most Australian sports involving a ball have been

handed down by the British Commonwealth but not all of them. Cricket, of course, is English but the Aussies have adopted it as their national sport. They compete on every level from schoolboy sports to International Test Cricket, played among the Commonwealth countries. Australia's rivals include the West Indies (known as the Windies), Pakistan, India, New Zealand and Mother England, along with African countries touched by British rule.

Simply (and that's the only way I would dare to explain it), cricket is played with a bat held by a **batsman** (not a batter as in baseball). The hard ball, traditionally red in color, is pitched or **bowled** by a **bowler** (no pitcher). The **pitch** refers to the packed running surface beneath the bowler's feet. The **wicket** consists of three wooden sticks standing upright called **stumps** with two **bails** or small wooden dowels across the top.

The bowler aims at the wicket and tries to knock the bails off, while the batsman tries to slap the ball away with a flat bat held low to the ground. If the bowler knocks the bails off, the batsman is out. As in baseball, the batsman can be caught out on a fly. Actually there are two batsmen on the **oval** (named for the shape of the field) simultaneously; but, I'll let someone else explain the nitty-gritty to you. To try to learn more without actually watching a match would be confusing.

Let me add that a **test match,** which is technically one game, continues over five days with a 40-minute lunch break and a 20-minute afternoon tea break every day. Imagine sitting from 11 A.M. to 6 P.M. for five consecutive days waiting for the outcome of one game!

In these less gracious modern times, people want to see more cricket played in shorter periods of time. So, an Aussie businessman helped create **one-day cricket** played by teams dressed in colored uniforms (not the traditional sporting white). The one-day games were perfect for television but the International Test Matches will always be the most important games of the year.

The first cricket batter is called the **opening batsman.** A big name batsman is as well known in Australia as Joe DiMaggio is in America. Therefore the name of a batsman gets dragged into idiomatic slang. You may hear someone at a **barby** ask, "Pass the **Colin Mc Donald.**" He does not want the player handed to him, he wants a bottle opener. Colin McDonald equals opening batsman or opener!

Ever heard of a **sticky wicket?** Perhaps you heard it in an old movie and wondered what on earth they were talking about and where did such a saying come from. The answer: cricket, of course! It means the ground around the wickets is wet or muddy. Now it is a euphemism for any "messy or difficult situation." A **good wicket** is just the opposite—advantageous.

In most cities you can pick the cricket oval by the initials C.G. They stand for **cricket ground.** Hence, they play cricket at the M.C.G. (The Melbourne Cricket Ground) or the S.C.G. (The Sydney Cricket Ground). But Brisbane will throw you. Queenslanders like being different. While they compete at a place formally named the Brisbane Cricket Ground on maps and tourist pamphlets, no one in Australia calls it that. The stadium stands in a suburb named Woolloongabba, so the cricket ground is always referred to as **The Gabba.** Nothing else.

Since cricket fields are rather large sporting arenas, other games and events can be played there too, including football. While Australians play rugby and soccer, there's only one game they call football, **Australian Rules football.** Colloquially, it's **Aussie rules** or just

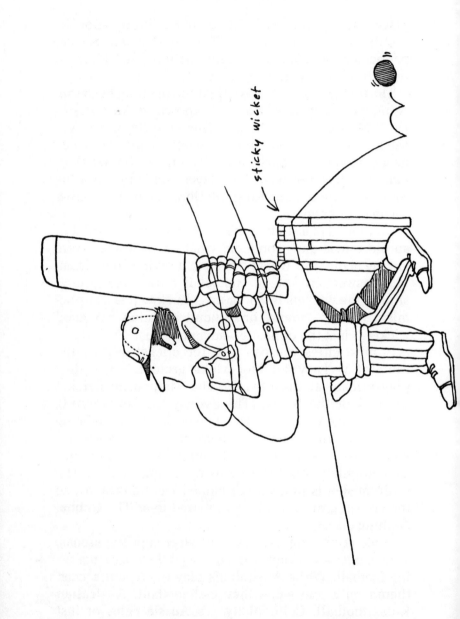

sticky wicket

plain **footy.** Footy has been mentioned in other sections of this book because it is **dinky-di** Australian. (Dinky-di rides the same road as **fair dinkum,** meaning honest or true blue.)

Because Aussie Rules bears the title "football," the Australians needed another heading for the American game. To them U.S. football with helmets and all the padded paraphenalia is **gridiron.** With the exception of an egg-shaped ball and a large playing field, the two sports have very little in common.

The 18 players on a **footy** side never stop. The game runs for 100 minutes, divided into four 25-minute quarters (which can be extended at the umpires' discretion). At the half, there is a 20-minute break. The play really never stops unless a stretcher must be brought onto the field to move an injured player. Otherwise, injuries get treated right on the field while the match continues around the man and the medic!

Footy is a winter sport, played from March through September, though to look at their uniforms you would not think so. Footy players dress like soccer and rugby players, in shorts and sleeveless jerseys, called **footy jumpers.** They do not wear any protective padding or headgear. That's not to say they couldn't use some protection, but it's just **not on!** Some say that would detract from the raw beauty of the play. To the untrained eye, it looks like chaos on the oval!

Like American football, a team wins by scoring goals. But there are four goal posts on each end, two tall inside posts and two shorter **behind** posts. A player gets six points for a goal and one point for **behinds.** To score a goal worth six points, a player has to kick a ball clearly between the two big posts without it being touched by another player. If another player touches it or if the ball hits a post on its way through, it only scores one point.

The raucous crowds at Aussie Rules' matches would not be complete without **hoons** and **larrikans** toting their share of **stubbies** and **brownies** (both are short brown bottles), **tinnies, T.T.s** and **tubes. Tinnies** and **T.T.'s** stem from the days when cans were made of tin, not **aluminium. Tubes** is modern slang for *can*. Remember **barrackers** (not rooters) are the fans of footy and all sports. They don their team colors in the form of woolly hats and scarves in the winter, and other things in the summer.

They wrap up the footy season in September. Their version of the Superbowl is the **Grand Final.** The state of Victoria, home of footy, where the majority of the teams are located, goes wild! All the talk is **Grand Final fever!**

Track and field events are popular, too, especially in school competitions. But, the sports category is not "track and field" as Americans call it. The category is **athletics.**

A lefty or southpaw in Australia bears the moniker **molly-dooker,** but I really don't know why. And the player, in any sport, recognized as the team's most valuable performer will be presented with the **"best and fairest"** award. It takes the place of the M.V.P.

Women play a version of basketball in Oz, called **netball.** It has seven players on each side and they pass the ball a lot like women's basketball once did. It's a popular club sport usually played on outdoor courts.

The bowling played indoors on wooden alleys had to be renamed, just like gridiron, because of the game known as **bowls.** The American game is **ten-pin bowling.** Theirs is a version of lawn bowls imported from the British Isles. The bowlers (not to be confused with the cricketers and the ten-pin players) roll balls on grass at bowling clubs where most members are retirees or **pensioners.** This kind of bowling is similar to the Italian game of boccie, which is played only with balls, not pins or clubs.

While cricket fills the bill as national sport, Australia's second greatest spectator sport is horse racing. Horse racing means gambling. So really the sport is **punting. Punters** bet. Any race day is labeled a **race meeting** or a **derby** (pronounced darby).

The race of the year is the **Melbourne Cup.** In many ways it's the equivalent of the Kentucky Derby, but unlike the Run for the Roses, Melbourne Cup Day is a holiday. Melbourne closes down so everyone can dress up and go to Flemington Race Course.

Traditionally, track members and their guests dress in their fanciest clothes and women try to outdo each other with the grandest outfits and finest hats. Every society columnist and fashion editor in the country descends on Flemington to see who is wearing what. You see, the race runs the first Tuesday in November and that may be the first glimpse of the summer fashion season.

Even if you are not a member, you can still go to Flemington and have a tailgate party in the parking lot. The folks who do that do not dress in *haute couture* like the members; instead, they go in **fancy dress. Fancy dress** means costumes. People outdo each other with the wildest hats and headgear. Whether inside or outside the gates, the champagne flows and everyone has a wonderful time.

Now, if you are not in Melbourne for Cup Day, you can probably attend a Melbourne Cup party at a nearby pub or racecourse which will have closed-circuit TV of the Cup races and local races as well. No one is left out.

In some places, casino gambling has been legalized. The favorite pastime inside the clubs can be summed up in one phrase: the **pokies.** That's the pet name for **poker machines,** better known to us as one-armed bandits or the slots.

Just like American kids, Aussie boys and girls have their unofficial sports. **Billycart** racing sits atop the list like the carts do atop a hill at the starting line. **Billycarts** closely resemble homemade go-carts. Somehow **billy** edged into the seat of another word, sat down and stayed forever. After all, wouldn't it be as easy to call them just plain carts?

When not rolling along in billycarts, you will probably find kids pedaling **pushbikes. Pushbikes** do not differ from other kinds of bicycles. It's just a compound word that came from pushing pedals. So, bikes and pushbikes, carts and billycarts are two sets of twins.

The Boxing Kangaroo

The **boxing kangaroo** became the symbol of Australia's sporting prowess on a summer's day in 1983 in the waters off Newport, Rhode Island, when the America's Cup challenger, *Australia II,* raised a huge flag with a golden kangaroo sporting red boxing gloves. *Australia II* went on to win the America's Cup yacht races that year, wresting the prized treasure from the U.S. which had held the trophy for 132 years.

Back home, the proud "boxing kanga" flag quickly flew everywhere, and now can be seen at all Australian international sporting events. It stands for strength and persistence in the arena, on the water, or on the track.

Beyond that, the history of the boxing kangaroo seems a bit blurred. It has been around for generations. Carnival acts promoted boxing kangaroos but certainly real live animals sparring in the ring were rarely seen

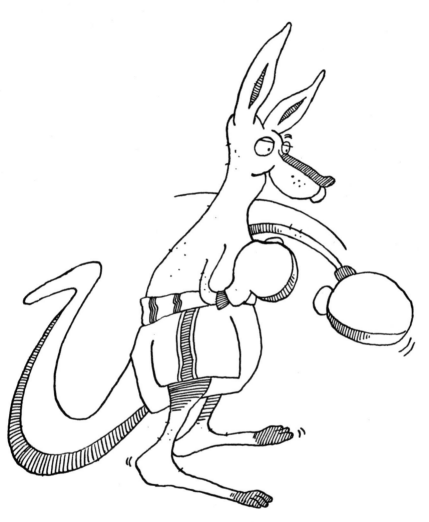

the mythical boxing kangaroo

Down Under. Maybe the concept comes from the movements of the kangaroos themselves. Since they stand on their huge back legs, their shorter forearms are free for other things than support. In the wild you will see playful kangaroos push each other around with their paws, so maybe that's where the idea came from.

If seeing kangaroos box is on your itinerary for a trip Down Under, sorry to disappoint you. It will not happen. The boxing kangaroo is a myth and a symbol, not a sport.

CHAPTER SEVEN

Pommies, Septics and Yanks

Aussies is the wonderful clipped version of *Australians* which the men and women Down Under proudly wear. It fits their style of informality. The stiff upper lip of the British wore thin when the penal colonies folded and the Aussies became an amalgamation of free immigrants looking for rich farming land, or gold, or just a less-congested place to live.

That informality carries over in their dealings with other countries. The general feeling that Australians "got it good" makes them a bit cocky (in the real definition of that word). Americans, for instance, have always been **Yanks.** The British called the early American colonists that and it has stuck. So the Aussies needed to create another handle for Yanks. Rhyming slang came to the rescue. Americans are **septics.** What a lovely term! Have you figured it out?

Septic tank rhymes with **Yank.** Americans are then **septic tanks,** shortened to **septics.** Perhaps at one time it was meant to be derogatory, but now it's all in fun.

Pommies are another story. All English people are called **poms** or **pommies** by the Aussies. The word descends from the days of convict transportation, or so legend has it. According to word-of-mouth tradition, the British subjects brought to the prison settlements of Australia were labeled "Prisoner of His Majesty" or P.O.M. But when life turned around and the Australians were guardians and rulers of their own land, they turned the ugly phrase on all other Brits still serving the crown. Now all British citizens are **pommies.** They know it and accept it, whether they like it is another matter.

The Macquarie Dictionary, considered by its publishers as an Australian achievement, and by others as *the* dictionary of the English language in Australia, cites the definition of **pommy** as "an Englishman," but adds that the origin of the word remains unknown. I suppose Macquarie lexicographers don't believe the legend.

New Zealanders have been burdened with a different brand, which they'll never shake either. To Australians their neighbors will always be **kiwis,** no matter what they do. **Kiwi,** in any form, relates to New Zealand just as kangaroos and koalas relate to Oz. The kiwi is a small flightless bird, native only to the islands of New Zealand, or **Kiwiland.**

In modern times people might think of the kiwi fruit as the origin of the handle hung on New Zealanders; but in a sense, it's the other way around. Because **kiwi** is associated with New Zealand so strongly, a bright

Septic Tank = Yank

marketing manager began to push the kiwi fruit on the world market. But, there was no fruit by that name. He made it up. The kiwi-fruit is the Chinese gooseberry which grows well in the New Zealand climate. You won't find the name kiwi-fruit referred to anywhere before the 1970s. Just one more example of how the kiwi, as a symbol, has permeated New Zealand life.

One other phrase sometimes denotes the **kiwi.** He might be called an **Enzed** or **Enzedder.** We are talking about New Zealanders here. **En** equals *N* and **zed** equals *Z.* Therefore, their name gets clipped to Enzed—a strange phrase.

Most other slang for nationalities is degrading, usually insults designed to describe a particular group of immigrants. Most are not much different from those thrown around the United States and therefore not worth mentioning.

A Visit to Honkers!

It may be an extension of "rock fever" that drives Australians to travel, especially those born after World War II. It's not unusual for babyboomers to take a year or longer off from work and leave Australia by boat or plane and find out what the rest of the world is doing. Because of widespread travel, favorite locations have been given nicknames understood by most people Down Under. The best ones are those close by (to them) in Southeast Asia.

A trip to Singapore is a "holiday in **Singers**" and a visit to Bangkok, Thailand, is a visit to **Bangers.** As an example of how commonplace these terms are, an airline adopted one in its slogan for trips to Hong Kong, a favorite shopping and business destination from Australia. The ad campaign for Cathay Pacific Airline picked up and used the colloquialism this way: "You'd be bonkers not to go via **Honkers!**" Honkers replaces Hong Kong. No kidding!

QANTAS

QANTAS, with its kangaroo logo, is the national government-run airline of Australia, but most foreigners do not understand the strange word QANTAS. No, it is not aboriginal and they do not drop the qu combination in Oz. QANTAS is an acronym for Queensland and Northern Territory Aerial·Service. Now you know. It's a great piece of trivia to stump your friends with.

Aussie Places

As we've said, Aussies call their own home OZ, so it's not a matter of throwing stones. Changes in the place name on a map don't stop there. Queensland, the Sunshine State, seems to bear the brunt of lots of linguistic fooling around. Queensland, being a hot state, works at a slower pace than New South Wales or Victoria, but there's plenty of work done there in the cane fields and on the pineapple and banana plantations. Because of that, Queensland stands tall as the **Banana Republic** and the people who live there must put up with the unattractive moniker **banana-benders.**

Brisbane (pronounced BRIZ-BIN) is the state capital, fondly known as **Brizzie,** and **Brizzie** residents are aptly called **Brizzie boys** and **Brizzie girls,** usually after they've moved elsewhere.

Queensland is not alone in the nickname category. Tasmania, originally called Van Dieman's Land under colonial rule, has fallen to the rewriters of the English language too. What sounds like a diminutive for the country's smallest state is just another clipped form. Tasmania is **Tassie** (pronounced Tazzie), a charming island which was once a prison.

Australia's largest city is Sydney. But that does not spare it from nicknames. Sydney falls to rhyming slang. The place was renamed **Steak and Kidney** long before anyone can remember. The residents of Sydney call themselves **Sydneysiders**.

Down in Melbourne, a town that has never been given a nickname, though historically it has had more than one name, people call themselves **Melburnians** and they pride themselves in their individual lifestyle distinct from that of Sydneysiders.

Any large city, however, retains the title **the big smoke.** That goes back to the early years of horsemen coming from a great distance who could tell a city was on the horizon by the smoke rising above it.

Three thousand miles away, across the great desert that divides Australia's coasts, known as the Nullarbor Plain, other destinations refuse to be left out of the nickname business, or to be left without an odd bit of local trivia that every visitor comes to recognize. The place is West Australia with its capital Perth.

Along the coast, you may hear people talk about **the Doctor.** He arrives promptly every afternoon and stirs the place up. The so-called **Doctor** is neither man nor beast. The Doctor depicts the wind that blows in from the Indian Ocean everyday at lunchtime. The wind was dubbed the Doctor because of its cooling, healing effect against the strong West Australian sun. But, while the Doctor does calm the temperature, he also blows the sand around, making the beautiful endless stretches of beaches hard to bear. The Doctor has become notorious among sailors because the strong wind blowing toward the shore makes for heavy sailing conditions, and makes for some of the world's most exciting yacht racing.

Yachting history was made in West Australia in 1987

when a tiny port town, the stepchild of Perth, became the site of the first non-American America's Cup race. The place is **Free-oh!** That is the loving pseudonym for the town of Fremantle. The clipped sobriquet was in place long before competing sailors from around the world arrived to turn the sleepy little port into an international tourist haven. Funny, though, how **Free-oh** seems to fit the spirit of the place in modern times!

CHAPTER EIGHT

Kangas, Koalas and More . . .

Native animals and birds color a language and add a unique dimension to it. They create analogies that make us laugh at our way of doing things. They allow us to tell vividly how something looks just by adding the comparative in the animal kingdom. Without even realizing it, we employ such words and phrases all the time to help us get through the day.

What are these euphemisms and descriptive phrases bearing animals? Think a moment. Americans rely on the lowly skunk more than we care to admit. "He smells like a skunk!" Everyone knows what that means but there's more to the list: "I've been skunked by that rat." "As drunk as a skunk." "That skunk left me high and dry." Our *skunk* phrases mean nothing Down

Under. A skunk to Aussies is the cartoon character Peppy Le Pew. Nothing more.

What about these phrases: "He's a bear of a man." "As quiet as a mouse." "Sly as a fox." "Strong as an ox." Every one of these phrases conjures up a specific meaning, with no further explanation necessary. They convey a detailed idea simply and easily. Many linguists may scorn them as clichés but where would our spoken language be without them?

Australian-English measures up exactly the same way, reliant on its furry and not so furry friends for a bit of linguistic spark in the language. Aussies have a rich variety of unusual mammals, reptiles, fish and fowl from which to choose their victims. The analogies can get lost on strangers who cannot picture the animal in the wild and, therefore, cannot understand what the descriptive phrase tries to evoke.

This chapter will introduce the reader to the marvelous and wondrous world of Australia's animal kingdom, filled with some of the world's oldest species; and even more importantly for our purposes, the chapter will explain their special place in Aussie-English.

Kangaroos and **koalas** epitomize Australia's uniqueness to most Americans. The strange animals which carry their babies in pouches seem set aside by nature, left in a pure habitat. The animals arouse interest because they are so different from anything anywhere else in the world. Most people are surprised to learn how many species of marsupials (pouched mammals) exist, ranging from tiny mice-like creatures to the giant kangaroo which can stand eye to eye with a man. Let's expel some myths about these unusual creatures as we learn more about the natural inhabitants of **Terra Australis.**

First, a koala is not a bear. The long-clawed tree

climber does not eat meat, a boring animal when it comes to food. Its entire diet is composed of leaves from certain kinds of eucalyptus trees, commonly called **gum trees** in Australia. The koala gets "high" on the leaves and spends most of his time sleeping in trees above the ground. One nickname for the koala is **Billy Bluegum.** A blue gum, with its bluish-grey bark is among a large variety of eucalyptus trees. Other gums include: red gums, rose gums, ghost gums, and others.

Kangaroos, the largest marsupial, have a number of compatriots in the bush who are often mistaken for kangas. The **Wallaby** and **Wallaroo** graze on golden grass just as kangaroos do but they are smaller than **roos.** Wallabies tend to have muscular forelimbs and, in many cases, live in rougher terrain. The baby kangaroo or any other similar animal baby is called a **joey.**

Because kangas are so prevalent throughout the Australian continent, they hold a large corner on the language as well. A man may be criticized for having **"kangaroos in the top paddock."** It means he's a little crazy. It stands as the equivalent of having "bats in the belfry."

There's also the seldom used verb **to kangaroo.** Since kangaroos do a kind of hop, the verb describes a jerky move, specifically to jerk a car, like someone learning to drive a stick shift.

Kangaroo can be found on the rhyming slang list, too. *Kangaroo* rhymes with *screw* but not *screw* as in *nuts and bolts.* Kangaroo means "screw" as in a prison guard, the bad guy to the inmates.

Leaving Australia, you might fly the **kangaroo route** from Sydney to London. And, as we've already explained, if you wind up on the **wallaby track** you might be lost forever.

The **quokka** (there's a new word for Scrabble) resides

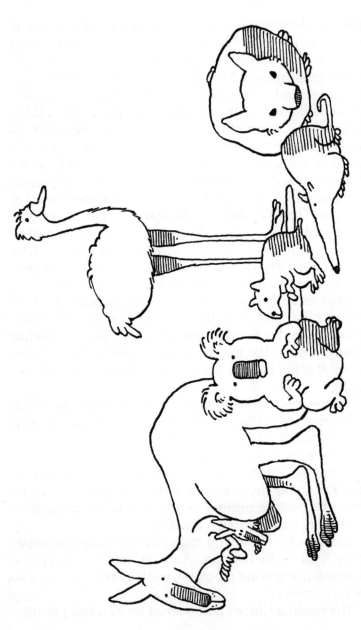

kanga, koala, quokka, emu, bandicoot, wombat

on Rottnest Island off the coast of Perth in West Australia. The first settlers mistook the little quokka for a big rat and named the island Rottnest, meaning rats' nest. Again, the quokka does not belong to the rodent family; it is a marsupial like its kangaroo cousin. The **quoll** was once mistaken for a small native cat, but it is not feline. It is another marsupial, as are most Aussie animals mentioned here.

Numbats and **wombats** sound like cartoon characters. But they are alive and well and living Down Under, too. The numbat is an anteater with stripes or bands on its body. A wombat is a furry, chubby noctural animal who burrows big holes beneath the ground. Wombats are the size of small pigs. Because the wombat is a nighttime animal, much like a cumbersome oversized mole, it is virtually blind in the sunlight. So, colloquially, if you are as "blind as a bat" you can be as **"blind as a wombat"** as well.

Most of us have heard of an opposum. But did you know the North American opossum is the only marsupial or pouched mammal on the continent and is a direct cousin of the Down Under inhabitants? Aussies' official name for opossums is **possums.** While North America has only one species of 'possum, Australia has heaps of possums.

Of course, their natural habitat is the bush, Australia's version of the countryside, but many species have made themselves quite comfortable in the modern suburbs and can be seen in backyard trees. Possums have adjusted so well, many people compare their suburban existence to that of squirrels in the neighborhood. They move about, from tree to tree, wire to wire, and roof to roof the way squirrels do, but they are bigger animals. So, if you would not want squirrels

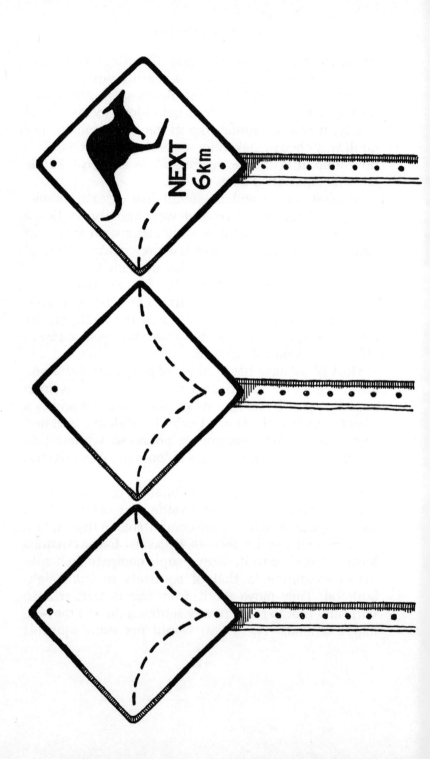

nestled in your attic for the winter, you certainly would not want possums living up there.

The common possum settled nicely into the lexicon too. Anyone as "happy as a possum up a gum tree" has had a very good day. Everything's rosy! Possums are known for their antics, jumping about and scurrying after each other. That knowledge explains why a bloke getting bored at a party might coax his mates to **stir the possums!** He wants to liven things up and get people moving. Possums may be described as rather cute and cuddly. (Not the American ones!) An Aussie daddy might call his little girl "Possum" or "Possie" as an endearment.

Marsupials with particularly odd-sounding names include: **bettongs, dunnarts, wuhl-wuhls, potoroos and bandicoots.** Ah, the bandicoot! He has suffered a great deal of torment under the Aussie language-makers. A bandicoot does not stand out as a particularly interesting creature on his own, but his name can be found scattered throughout colloquial and euphemistic speech.

The bandicoot is a bow-legged hairless little creature with skin similar to that of a Mexican hairless dog. So, a bald man gets described as "bald as a bandicoot." Anyone with bowlegs lives with a similar description: "legs like a bandicoot" or **bandy-legged.**

Since the little bandicoot scurries about something like a prairie dog, any slightly crazy person might be labeled "as barmy as a bandicoot," right up there with having "kangaroos in the top paddock." But if someone's been outcast, he is "like a bandicoot on a burnt ridge," alone and forlorn. The list of rejects does not end there. A man may be as "lousy as a bandicoot" which means he's been dubbed a miser. The old-fashioned verb **to bandicoot** meant to steal potatoes, just like a bandicoot does for his dinner. Somewhere along the way, you might hear about a **bilby,** a species of bandicoot with long rabbit-like ears.

Two really strange little mammals live in a category all their own. The **echidna,** a spiny anteater similar to a porcupine in looks, and the **platypus,** considered an example of God's sense of humor. The features of a platypus come from many animals—a bill like a duck, a tail like a beaver and feet like an otter. Both are monotremes, the only mammals known to man that lay eggs, hatch their young, and raise them in a pouch where they suckle mother's milk.

The **dingo** denotes the wild dog of Australia believed to be descended from the early dogs first brought there by the aboriginals who founded the continent to the south. The dingo is a scavenger, a roamer who lives in packs, much like the coyote. One location of dingo on the vocabulary is under verbs: **to dingo** means "to rat" on or tattle on. When a bloke calls another "a dingo," he means he's gutless.

Like the dingo, the **brumby** can trace its ancestry to other continents before man settled on **Terra Australis.** What is a **brumby?** The word distinguishes the wild horses of Australia from those any place else in the world. The brumbies of the high plains have their own mystique, like the mustangs of the American West— they are believed untrainable except by the best horse-handlers in the district. A poem by "Banjo" Patterson and the film *The Man from Snowy River* depict a young stockman chasing the brumby mob in a dynamic feat.

We've already discussed some of the domestic animals that have been renamed Down Under. The **chook** and the **bobby calf** both live on the station, serving man. The **chook** is any full-grown chicken and the

bobby calf is the young veal calf. An "old biddy" might be called "a silly old chook."

The sheep raised in Australia for the world's finest wool are the merino. Clothing makers and sheepskin manufacturers seek out merino for its high quality. So, if a guy is top notch, the nicest bloke in town, he's **pure merino.**

Any sheep may be referred to as a **jumbuck.** The *Macquarie Dictionary* cites the etymology as an "aboriginal corruption of *jump up.*" When herded, sheep do jump.

FURLESS FRIENDS

A non-mammal with four legs is the **goanna,** a variety of hulking monitor lizard. The word *goanna* probably stems from a bastardization of *iguana.* Aussies bill **goanna salve** as a household remedy, standing on the medicine cabinet shelf alongside eucalyptus oil.

A uniquely talented musician might even play the **goanna.** Not the lizard. In rhyming slang, goanna rhymes with "pianna." The poor elegant piano gets reduced to this, the object of a rhyme and a bad rhyme at that!

The goanna's slippery rellies include **Joe Blakes.** Watch out for Joe Blakes in the grass because many of them are deadly poisonous in Australia. Do you know what we are looking for? Think rhyming slang. Joe Blakes rhymes with *snakes!* So keep looking down, or up for that matter; he may be hanging from a tree.

Other rhymes swim in the ocean and bring just as much fear to the hearts of man as do the venomous Joe Blakes. Swimmers or surfers can clear a beach with the cry, **"Noahs!"** They haven't seen the ghost of Noah's Ark, but they are screaming about the rhyming partner of Noah's Ark. The cry elsewhere might be "Sharks in the water!" Surely, that will empty a beach. Of course, a good portion of Australia's beaches are protected by shark fences or shark nets to keep them from the bathing and surf areas, but the nets are not found everywhere and sharks like the same warm water people do.

More marine animals float through the language. The shrimp's cousin, the tasty **prawn** adds a tang to the tongue. "Don't **come the raw prawn** with me!" someone says with a scowl. He means do not try to impose your foolish ideas on me; don't dish up "that baloney." The phrase may be shortened to "Don't **come at that**." But if someone says, "Don't be a **raw prawn**," that person is telling you not to act like an idiot.

Speaking of swimming, the trout gets into the idiom act too. When someone gets called a **trout mouth**, it's not flattering at all. It means he's a big mouth, but more than that, he's the guy that cannot shut up, the one who spreads a secret he's been told to keep quiet.

Birds

Birds fly through the language, migrating from one term to another as easily as they go from tree to tree. Our feathered friends, some beautiful, some ordinary, have helped rewrite the common cackle of Oz.

The first example we've seen in this book is the **cocky**. A **cocky** stands for any kind of farmer. (See Chapter Four for a complete list of cockies.) The descriptive word is taken from the beautiful yellow-crested bird, the **cockatoo**. As a verb, **to cockatoo** means to scratch the dirt for a living or dirt farm. But a cockatoo may also be a sentinel, warning of approaching danger.

You know those days when you wake up and your mouth has a terrible taste in it, maybe it's leftover from what you ate or drank the night before. The Aussies drag the pet cockatoo into the description. "I've got a mouth like the bottom of a cocky's cage!" Picture the bottom of a bird cage and you will now how bad that is.

The cockatoo's cousin the **galah** has scratched out its own niche in Aussie-English. The galah, known as the rosy-breasted cockatoo, has stunning coloring, a deep pink chest with soft grey wings and back—very flamboyant in the animal world! So, any person who dresses flashy or dresses up too much for the occasion gets baptized a galah, as in, "That bloke's a bloody galah." By the way, the word is not pronounced like *gala*. It's "ga-LAH."

The **emu** reminds most people of an ostrich. Australia's tall flightless bird lays teal-green eggs, and shares the official Commonwealth seal with the kangaroo. Take a look, if you have a chance.

A funny "emu term" in the lexicon embodies the Australian sense of humor—**emu-bobbing.** It has nothing to do with emus, of course. Farmers and developers clear land in Australia by burning off the scrub and trees. Afterwards, branches and large twigs get left behind. So, the boss sends out the **emu-bobbers** to pick up the pieces. The phrase is an analogy. The workers moving about with their heads down and bottoms up personify emus scratching for food.

The **kookaburra** sits tall as the king of the bush; it is a species of kingfisher. Its piercing laugh-like call has become synonymous with the sounds of Australia's countryside and backyard scenes. No barby would be complete without being punctuated by the kookaburra's call.

Another common bird found everywhere in Australia is the black and white **magpie**. A magpie is similar to a large crow. Aussies also call it a bower bird because it steals any colorful bits and scraps that it can carry to its nest for decoration. Now, a euphemism coined to describe a petty thief is, as you guessed, a **bower bird.**

We've had lists of words in Chapter Four that creatively depict the imaginary place beyond the Outback, beyond the Black Stump. One more phrase should be added to that nomenclature: **"Where the crows fly backwards"** is in a place called "God-knows-where."

When you are down and out, you might feel like a **shag on a rock,** or an outcast. At a party, where you do not know a soul, you typify the **shag on a rock** (the outsider). A **shag** is a cormorant, a water bird who makes his lonely life on the craggy outcroppings of rocks along the sea. One other comparative employs the poor maritime fowl: **as wet as a shag!** Soaked to the bone.

Part Two

Two separate glossaries are supplied in this section of *Kangaroo's Comments and Wallaby's Words*. The first lists the Aussie words, phrases and expressions that have been found in bold print throughout the earlier chapters and will supply a brief American definition for the Australian term. It notes the chapter or chapters in which the term can be found so you can look back and get a better feel for the use (and abuse) of the word than is given by the simplified glossary definition.

The second glossary complements the first. There you will find lists of American words followed by their Aussie counterparts. This glossary is a bit shorter because it condenses all the Australian phrases with the same definition into groupings. Again, the chapter references accompany each Yank word or phrase, so the reader can go back into the chapters and get a better understanding of what that Aussie means.

Where you see (RS), it's pointing out phrases from Australian *Rhyming Slang* explained in Chapter One.

Australian-American

Aussie Term	Yank Meaning	Chapter
ABC, the	Australian Broadcasting Co.	4
a wander	a walk	4
aggro	aggravated	4
Akubra (brand)	stockmen's hat	5
Al Capone (RS)	phone	1
al-foil	aluminum foil	1,2
all in	exhausted	4
ambo	ambulance worker	1,3
anklebiter	small child	3
Anzacs, anzacs	soldiers, oatmeal cookies	2, 3
appetizers	second restaurant course	2
apple pie (RS)	sky	4
argy-bargy	argumentative	4

Aussie Term	Yank Meaning	Chapter
Arthur or Martha	"coming or going"	4
athletics	track and field	6
"Aunty"	the ABC	4
Aussie Rules	Australian Rules Football	1,6
Aussie Battler	hardworking underdog	3
Aussie salute	swatting flies	4
Australian flag	shirttail sticking out	5
avos	avocados	5
bab	babbler	3
babbling brook (RS)	cook	1,3
back paddock	North 40	4
back of Bourke	God-knows-where	4
back of beyond	God-knows-where	4
backblocks	back streets	4
backing dog	sheep dog	4
backslang	to live as a hobo	3
baddie, bad lot	bad guy	3
bag of fruit (RS)	suit	1
bails	part of the cricket wicket	6
baked beans on toast	breakfast food	2
bald as a bandicoot	bald	8
Ballarat (RS)	cat	1
Banana-bender	Queenslander	7
Banana Republic, the	Queensland	7
bandicoot	a marsupial	8
bandy-legged	bowlegged	8
bang on	exactly	4
bangers	Bangkok, Thailand	7

Aussie Term	Yank Meaning	Chapter
bangers	sausages	2
Bappo	Baptist	3
barmy as a bandicoot	crazy	8
barney	a brawl	4
Barossa pearl (RS)	girl	3
barrack; barracker	to cheer, sports fan	4,6
barrister	lawyer	3
basinful of trouble	lots of trouble	4
bathers	swimsuit	5
batsman	batter in cricket	6
bay bug	like a small lobster	2
beaut!	terrific!	4
beetroot	red beets	2
behind	a goal point in footy	6
berk	bad person	3
best and fairest	most valuable player; M.V.P.	6
bettong	a marsupial	8
bibful	lots of gossip	4
Bible-basher	preacher	3
bickies	money	4
bikers	motorcycle riders	1
bikies	motorcycle gang members	1
bilby	a kind of bandicoot	8
billa	water	4
billabong	creek runoff	4
billy lids (RS)	kids	1
billy tongs	tongs for water pot	4
Billy Bluegum	koala	8
billy	water pot	1,4
billycan	water pot	4

Aussie Term	Yank Meaning	Chapter
billycart	go-cart	6
billytea	camp tea	4
bird	gal; chick	3
Birko (brand)	electric kettle	5
Biro (brand)	ballpoint pen	5
biscuits, bickies (food)	cookies	1,2
bitumen	asphalt	4
Bizzo!	nonsense	4
Black Stump	an imaginary place	4
black sauce	Worchestershire sauce	2
blind as a wombat	blind	8
Blinky Bill (RS)	silly	3
block of flats	apartment complex	5
bloke	guy	3
blowies; blowflies	flies	4,5
bludger	a do-nothing	3,4
blue; bluey	(many meanings)	3,4
board shorts	longer-legged swimsuits	6
board-boy	shedhand	4
boardies	surfers	6
Bob Hope (RS)	soap, dope	1
bob	a coin	4
bobby calf	veal calf	4,8
bodgie	1950s "greaser"	3
bogie	swimming hole	4
boiled lollies	hard candy	2
boiled shirt	a stuffed shirt	3
boil-up	a brawl	4
bollocks!	baloney!	4
bols	nude	4

Glossary: Australian-American Reference

Aussie Term	Yank Meaning	Chapter
bon-bons	holiday noise makers	1
bonnet (car)	car hood	5
bonzer!	terrific!	4
boo-ay	the boondocks	4
boomerang bender	tale teller	3
boomers	big waves	6
boot (car)	car trunk	5
bot	borrow/have	2
bottle-oh	bottle collector	1
bowler	pitcher in cricket	6
bowls	lawn bowling	6
boxing kangaroo	a sporting symbol	6
box-on	a brawl	4
brekky	breakfast	1,2
brickie	brick layer	1,3
Brizzie boys/girls	Brisbane residents	7
Brizzie	Brisbane	7
broomie	broomhand in a shearing shed	4
brownies	brown beer bottles, beer	6
brumby	wild horse	8
bubble and squeak	leftovers	2
buck's party or night	stag or bachelor party	5
big smoke, the	any city	7
Buckley's chance	no chance	4
bugger all	nothing	4
buggered	exhausted	4
bulletin	newscast	3
bullo!	baloney!	4
bullocky	nude	4

Aussie Term	Yank Meaning	Chapter
bullswool!	baloney!	4
bunny	"dumb bunny"	3
burl	leisurely drive	5
bush telegraph	the "grapevine"	5
bush, the	the outback	3
bushcook	stockman's cook	3
bush-cure	home remedy	5
bushie; bushman	anyone living in the bush	3
bushranger	outlaw	3,4
camp	"gay," homosexual	3
capsicums	peppers	5
Captain Cook (RS)	look	1
car park	parking lot	1
caravan	camper, R.V.	5
cardie	cardigan	5
Catho	Catholic	3
caulie	cauliflower	1
Cheers!	Bye!	4
cheese and kisses (RS)	Mrs.	1
chemist	pharmacist	3
cheque	check	1
Cherry Ripe (brand)	candy bar	2
chewie	chewing gum	2
Chiko Rolls (brand)	takeout snack	2
china plate (RS)	spouse, mate	1
chockie	chocolate	2
chook	chicken	4,8
Chrissy	Christmas	1
clothes pegs	clothespins	5
cocky	farmer	3,4,8
coffee lounge	luncheonette	2

Aussie Term	Yank Meaning	Chapter
Colin McDonald	a bottle opener	6
college	any private school	5
combi	camper-car in one	5
come a cropper	go to ruin	4
come good	get better	4
come the raw prawn	impose foolish ideas	8
compere	program host	3
Congo	Congregationalist	3
coo-ee!	bush call	4
cop the blue	get blamed	4
cordial	liquid Kool Aid	2
corn flour	cornstarch	5
corro students	correspondence students	1
corroboree	aboriginal celebration	4
cot	crib, bed	5
cozzie	swimsuit	5
crackers	holiday noise makers	1
crayfish	lobster	2
cricket ground	cricket stadium	6
crook	sick	5
crumpets	similar to English muffins	2
cuppa	a cup of . . .	2
daggy	outdated	4
dags	dirty wool	4
Dagwood dog	hot dogs on sticks	2
dam	waterhole	4
de facto	live-in boyfriend/ girlfriend	3

Aussie Term	Yank Meaning	Chapter
dead horse (RS)	ketchup (tomato sauce)	2
deckie	boat's deckhand	3
derro	derrelict	3
Devvy tea	Devonshire tea, snack	2
dicky	unsteady	4
didgeridoo	aboriginal wind instrument	4
digger	buddy; miner	3
diggeress	miner's wife	3
dilly (RS)	silly	3
dillybag	carry sack	4
dim sim	dim sum	2
dingo	species of wild dog, or gutless person	8
dinkum	honest	4
dinky-di	true blue	2
divvy van	paddy wagon	1
doccos	documentaries	1
the Doctor	West Australia's wind	7
doing the ton	driving 100 m.p.h.	5
doing the block	showing off	5
Driz-a-Bone (brand)	stockmen's raincoat	5
drongo	stupid person	3
dry bickies	crackers	2
dunnart	a marsupial	8
dunny	outhouse	5
earbasher	talks your ear off	3
eau de cologne (RS)	phone	1
echidna	spiny anteater	8
electric jug	electric kettle	5

Glossary: Australian-American Reference

Aussie Term	Yank Meaning	Chapter
emu	flightless bird	8
emu-bobbing	collecting twigs	8
en suite	bedroom with attached bath	5
entree	first restaurant course	2
Enzed	New Zealander	7
Esky (brand)	ice chest; cooler	5
fag	cigarette	4
fair dinkum	honest	4
fair go	fair chance	4
fairy floss	cotton candy	2
fancy dress	costumes	6
Father Santa	Santa Claus	1
fillet	filet	2
first floor	2nd floor	5
fish 'n' chips	fried fish and fries	2
flaggie	flagman	3
flake	shark filet	2
flat block	apartment complex	5
flog the cat	complain lots	4
footy	Australian Rules Football	1,6
Fred; Blind Freddy	character	3
Free-oh	Fremantle, W.A.	7
Friday week	a week from Friday	5
fringe	bangs (hair)	5
frog and toad (RS)	road	4
Front as big as Myer	a big facade	5
fronting the till	standing in front of the cash register	5
G'day!	Hello!	4
galah	rosy-breasted	8

Aussie Term	Yank Meaning	Chapter
	cockatoo, flashy dresser	
game as Ned Kelly	adventurous	4
garbo	garbage collector	1
gets into strife	finds trouble	3
goanna (RS)	piano	8
goanna salve	household remedy	8
goanna	a monitor lizard	8
golden syrup	sweet breakfast syrup	2
gone off	turned rotten	2
Good on Ya!	You've done well!	4
Grand Final, the	footy superbowl	6
grazier	rancher, farmer	3,4
greasy wool	wool with lanolin	5
greenies	environmentalists	1
grey ghost	parking cop, meter maid	3
gridiron	American football	6
griller, grilled	broiler, broiled	2
Grouse!	Terrific!	4
gum tree	eucalyptus tree	8
gumbies, gumboots	rubber boots	5
happy as Larry	thrilled	4
Happy Jack's (TM)	Burger King	2
happy as a possum. . .	very happy	8
heaps	lots of	2
hen's party	bridal shower	5
Hill's Hoist (brand)	clothesline	5
holidays	vacation	1
hollies	holidays	1
hollow log (RS)	dog	1

Glossary: Australian-American Reference

Aussie Term	Yank Meaning	Chapter
holly house	vacation house	1
home paddock	field around house	4
Honkers	Hong Kong	7
hooly-dooly!	Holy cow!	4
hoons	loud-mouth ruffians	3
Hooroo!	Bye!	4
hostie; hostess	stewardess	3
hotting up	heating up	4
housing estate	housing development	5
How's your father?	(derogatory adjective)	4
hump bluey	carry a bedroll	3
humpy	mud hut	4
iced coffee	drink, but different	2
Jack Shay	camp pot	4
jackeroo (jackaroo)	stockman	3
Jacky Howe	sleeveless wool shirt	5
jaffas (brand)	candy balls	2
jaffle iron	sandwich maker	2
jaffle	sandwich	2
jam	jam or jelly	2
jelly	gelatin	2
Joe Blakes (RS)	snakes	8
John Hops (RS)	cops	1
journos	journalists	1
jumbuck	a sheep	8
jumper	pullover, sweater	5
just a tick	wait a minute	5
kangaroo (RS)	"screw," a prison guard	8
kangaroo	largest marsupial	8

Aussie Term	Yank Meaning	Chapter
kangaroos in the top paddock	crazy	8
kerb	curb	1
khaki (say "car-key")	khaki	3
kindie	kindergarten	5
Kiwi	New Zealander	7
knickers	panties	5
koala	a marsupial	8
kookaburra	laughing bird	8
lamington, lam	a coconut covered mini-cake	2
larrikans	loud-mouth ruffians	3
lay-by	lay away plan	5
leadlight	stained glass	5
lemonade	lemon-flavored soda or pop	2
lesbo	lesbian	3
Lilo (brand)	inflatable raft	6
littlies	little children	5
lollies	candy	2
loo	toilet	5
lounge room	living room	5
mad keen	crazy about	6
magpie	crow-like bird	8
main course	main dish	2
make a blue	make a mistake	4
Manchester	linens	5
mate	pal, buddy	3
Matilda	a bedroll	3
meat pie	kind of pot pie	2
Melbourne Cup, the	Australia's top horse race	1 to 6

Aussie Term	Yank Meaning	Chapter
Melburnians	Melbourne residents	7
Metho	Methodist	3
Mick	Catholic	3
mickey calf	wild veal calf	4
milk bar	small grocery	2
milko, milkoh	milkman	1
minced meat	chopped meat	2
Minties (brand)	chewy mint candy	2
mister	surgeon	3
mob	flock, crowd	4
moleskins	bush pants	5
molly-dooker	lefty	6
more-ish	makes you want more	2
morning tea, afternoon tea	coffee break equivalent	2
mozzies	mosquitoes	4
mucks it up	messes things up	5
mudguards	fenders	5
muesli	granola	2
mushies	mushrooms	5
Myer	department store	5
'nanas	bananas	5
napkins, nappies	diapers	5
nark	bad person	3
Ned Kelly	legendary outlaw	3,4
netball	a version of basketball	6
never-never, the	the boondocks	4
never-never plan	credit plan	4
news presenter	anchorperson	3
no worries	nothing to worry	4

Aussie Term	Yank Meaning	Chapter
	about	
Noah's (Ark) (RS)	shark	8
Norm	character	3
Not on!	There's no way	3,6
numbat	a marsupial	8
nursing	cuddling	5
ocker	a redneck	3
off to Billyo	God-knows-where	4
on the nose	rotten smelling	2
opening batsman	first batter in cricket	6
Oxford scholar (RS)	dollar	1
Oz	Australia to Aussies	1
paddock	field	4
panel beater	auto body shop	5
pasties	takeout snack	2
pastoralist	rancher	3,4
Pat Malone (RS)	alone	1
pavlova, pav	a meringue-like dessert	2
pellets	small pieces of gum	2
pensioners	senior citizens, retirees	6
petrol	gasoline	5
pie warmer	mini-heating oven	2
pie and peas	pot pie with peas	2
pikelets	kind of pancakes	2
pimp	tattletale	3
pinnies, pinafores	ladies' jumpers	5
pitch	surface beneath the cricket bowler	6
plastic flower (RS)	shower	1
plats	braids	5
platypus	an aquatic mammal	8

Glossary: Australian-American Reference

Aussie Term	Yank Meaning	Chapter
poddy lamb	hand-fed lamb	4
poddy calf	hand-fed calf	4
pokies, poker machines	slot machines	6
pollies	politicians	1
polo collar	turtleneck	5
Pommy, Poms	Englishman, Englishmen	7
poofter	a "gay" man	3
poon	recluse	3
port	schoolbag	5
possie (pozzie)	position, place	1
possum	a marsupial	8
postie	postman	1
potoroo	a marsupial	8
prang	an accident	5
prawn	shrimp	2,8
prawn cutlets	fried shrimp	2
Presbo	Presbyterian	3
Pressbutton	Presbyterian	3
prezzies	presents, gifts	1
public schools	private schools	5
pumpkin (butternut, etc.)	squash	2
punch-up	a brawl	4
punters, punting	bettors, betting	6
pure merino	top of the line	8
pushbike	bicycle	6
Qantas	the Australian airline	7
queue, queuing up	line, lining up	5
quid	a coin	4
quokka	a marsupial	8

Aussie Term	Yank Meaning	Chapter
quoll	a marsupial	8
R.M. Williams (brand)	bush clothier	5
Rafferty's rules	no rules	4
rapt	thrilled	4
raw prawn	idiot	8
reffo	refugee	3
reggo	car registration	5
rellies, relos	relatives	1
Rice Bubbles (brand)	Rice Krispies	2
rides like billyo	rides like the wind	4
ringer	top shearer	4
Ripper!	Terrific!	4
roadhouse	diner (sort of)	2
root	(foul slang)	4
ropeable	fit to be tied	4
roses are red (RS)	bread	2
Royal Show, the	state fair	4
rubbers	pencil erasers	5
sandshoes	sneakers	5
sanger	sandwich	2
sauce, tomato sauce	ketchup; catsup	2
sausage rolls	takeout snack	2
Saveloys, Savs (brand)	hot dogs	2
savories	hors d'oeuvres	2
scones	biscuits	2
septic tanks (RS)	Yanks	7
serviettes	napkins	5
shag on a rock	outcast	8
She's sweet!	Everything's great!	4
She's apples!	Everything's great!	4

Glossary: Australian-American Reference

Aussie Term	Yank Meaning	Chapter
shearing shed	where sheep are shorn	4
shed	barn, outbuilding	4
sheila	woman, girl	3
she'll be right	It'll be okay.	4
shiny bottom	clerk or secretary	3
shout	pay for someone's drink, your round	2
showbags	kids' sample bags	4
silverbeet	Swisschard	2
Singers	Singapore	7
sister	nurse	3
sit up like Jacky	stand proud	4
skivvy	cotton turtleneck	5
sloppy joe	sweatshirt	5
slouch hat, slouchie	soldier's hat	3
Smarties (brand)	like M&M's	2
smoko	a break from work	4,5
snag, the	stockman's cook	3
snags	sausages	2
soda	soda water	2
solicitor	lawyer	3
spaghetti on toast	breakfast food	2
spanner	wrench	5
spider	a soda fountain drink	2
spot on	exactly	4
spring rolls	egg rolls	2
spruiker	hawker	3
squash (lemon or orange)	soda	2
squiz	quick look	4
starkers	nude	4

Aussie Term	Yank Meaning	Chapter
state schools	public schools	5
station	ranch	3,4
Steak and Kidney	Sydney	1,7
sticky wicket	messy situation	6
sticky beaks	nosey-bodies	4
stir the possums!	liven it up	8
stoush	a brawl	4
Stubbies (brand)	work shorts, beer bottles	6
stuffed	(foul slang)	4
stumps	part of the cricket wicket	6
sundowner	itinerant worker	3
surf carnivals	lifeguard competitions	6
Surf Lifesaving Club (S.L.C.)	volunteer lifeguards	6
surfies	surfers	6
swag it	live as an itinerant	3
swaggie, swagman	itinerant, hobo	3,4
sweet bickies	cookies	2
sweets	desserts	2
Sydney or the bush	all or nothing	4
Sydneysiders	Sydney residents	7
take the mickey out	tease	4
take a sticky beak	be nosy	4
takeaway	takeout food	2
tall poppy	well-known achiever	4
Tassie	Tasmania	7
tea	supper	2
tea rooms	small restaurants	2
telly	television	1

Glossary: Australian-American Reference

Aussie Term	Yank Meaning	Chapter
ten-pin bowling	American-style bowling	6
Terra Australis	Australia	8
terrace houses	row houses	5
test match	five-day-long cricket game	6
Texta (brand)	marking pen	5
till	cash register	5
tinny	lucky	4
tinny, T.T.s	can of beer, "traveling tinnies"	1,2,3,6
tit-for-tat (RS)	hat	1,6
to dingo	to tattle	8
to kangaroo	move jerkily	8
toey	jumpy	4
togs	swimsuit	5
tonnes	tons	1
tracks	driveways	4
trammies	tram drivers	1
transportees	convict settlers	4
treacle	cane syrup	2
trouble and strife (RS)	wife	1
trout mouth	big mouth	8
truckies	truck drivers	1
tubes	beer cans	6
tucker	food	2
tuckerbag	lunch bag	2
tuckerbox	food box	2
tuckshop	snack bar	2
two-bob watch, crazy as a. . .	crazy	4

KANGAROO'S COMMENTS AND WALLABY'S WORDS

Aussie Term	Yank Meaning	Chapter
Tyke	Catholic	3
tyre	tire	1
uni students	co-eds	1
uni	university	1,5
up the boo-ay	the boondocks	4
ute, utility wagon	car/truck combination	5
Veedub	V.W., Volkswagen	5
Vegemite (brand)	Aussie snack	2
veranda	any porch	5
Violet Crumble (brand)	candy bar	2
walkabout	wander away	4
wallaby track	God-knows-where	4,8
wallaby	a marsupial	8
wallaroo	a marsupial	8
Wally Grout	shout, your round of drinks	2
Warwick Farms (RS)	arms	1
Wellies, Wellingtons	rubber boots	5
wet as a shag	soaking wet	8
Wettex (brand)	spongy cloth	5
where the crow flies backwards	God-knows-where	8
whinge	complain	4
white goods	major appliances	5
wicket	pitcher's target in cricket	6
willy-willy	wind funnel	4
windcheater	sweatshirt	5
within coo-ee	within the sound of your voice	4
wombat	a marsupial	8

Aussie Term	Yank Meaning	Chapter
Woolies	Woolworth's	4
woolshed hop	barn dance	4
woolshed	where sheep are shorn	4
woop woop	God-knows-where	4
wuhl-wuhl	a marsupial	8
yabbies	crayfish	2
yakker, hard yakker	work	4
Yank tank	big American car	5
Yanks	Americans	7
your kick	money, kitty, wallet	5
zambuck	first-aid attendant	3
zed	the letter zee	1

GLOSSARY TWO

American-Australian

Yank Term	Aussie Expression	Chapters
a look	Captain Cook (RS)	1
achiever	tall poppy	4
aggravated	aggro, ropeable	4
all or nothing	Sydney or the bush	4
alone	Pat Malone (RS)	1
ambulance driver	ambo	1,3
American car	Yank tank	5
American	Yank, septic (RS)	7
apartment complex	flat block, block of flats	5
argumentative	argy-bargy	4
arms	Warwick Farms (RS)	1
asphalt; paving	bitumen	4
Australia	Oz, the Antipodes, Terra Australis, the Land Down Under	1,8

Yank Term	Aussie Expression	Chapter
Australian Rules football	Aussie Rules, footy	1
auto body shop	panel beater	5
avocados	avos	5
back streets	backblocks	4
bad person	baddie, bad lot, berk, nark	3
bald	bald as a bandicoot	8
baloney	bollocks, bullo, bullswool	4
bananas	'nanas	5
Bangkok, Thailand	Bangers	7
bangs (hair)	fringe	5
Baptist	Bappo	3
barn	shed	4
bedroll	Matilda, bluey	4
beer	T.T.s, tinnies, tubes, stubbies, brownies	2,3,6
bettor	punter	6
bicycle	pushbike	6
big waves	boomers	6
big mouth	trout mouth	8
blind as a bat	blind as a wombat	8
boondocks, the sticks	boo-ay, the never-never, on the wallaby track, woop woop, back of beyond, back of Bourke, off to Billy-oh, where the crows fly	4,8

Glossary: American-Australian Reference

Yank Term	Aussie Expression	Chapter
	backwards	
borrow	bot	2
bottle opener	Colin Mac Donald	6
bowlegged	bandy-legged	8
bowling	ten-pin bowling	6
braids	plats	5
brawl	punch-up, stoush, box-on, barney, boil-up, blue	4
bread	roses are red (RS)	2
breakfast	brekky	2
bridal shower	hen's party	5
Brisbane residents	Brizzie boys/girls	7
Brisbane	Brizzie	7
broiler	griller	2
bucks (money)	bickies	4
Burger King	Happy Jack's	2
buy a round of drinks	shout	2
camper	combi; caravan	5
camper's teapot	billy	4
candy	lollies	2
car fenders	mudguards	5
car accident	prang	5
car registration	reggo	5
car trunk	boot	5
car hood	bonnet	5
cardigan	cardie	5
cash register	till	5
cat	Ballarat (RS)	1
Catholic	Catho, mick, tyke	3
check (banking)	cheque	1
chicken	chook	4,8

Yank Term	Aussie Expression	Chapter
child	littlie, anklebiter	3,5
chocolate	chockie	2
Christmas holidays	Hollies	1
Christmas	Chrissy	1
cigarette	fag	4
clothes pins	clothes pegs	5
clothesline	Hill's Hoist (brand)	5
coffee break	smoko, tea	4,5
college, university	uni	1,5
coming or going	Arthur or Martha	4
complain	whinge, flog the cat	4
Congregationalist	Congo	3
convict settlers	transportees	4
cook	babbling brook (RS), a snag	1,3
cookies	sweet biscuits	2
cooler, ice chest	Esky (brand)	5
cop	John Hop (RS)	1
cornstarch	corn flour	5
costume	fancy dress	6
cotton candy	fairy floss	2
crackers	dry biscuits	2
crayfish	yabbies	2
crazy	barmy as a bandicoot, crazy as a two-bob watch, kangaroos in the top paddock	4,8
crazy about, fanatical	mad keen	6
crib, bed	cot	5
cuddling	nursing	5

158

Glossary: American-Australian Reference

Yank Term	Aussie Expression	Chapter
cup of coffee or tea	cuppa	2,5
curb	kerb	1
desserts	sweets	2
diapers	napkins, nappies	5
diners	roadhouses	2
dingo	wild dog, gutless person	8
documentary	docco	1
dog	hollow log (RS)	1
dollar	Oxford scholar (RS)	1
driveways	tracks	4
electric kettle	electric jug, Birko (Brand)	5
Englishman	Pommy, Pom	7
environmentalist	greenie	1
erasers	rubbers	5
eucalyptus tree	gum tree	8
everything's great!	she's sweet, she's apples	4
exactly	spot on, bang on	4
exhausted	buggered, all in	4
fan of sports	barracker	4
farmer, rancher	cocky, grazier, pastoralist	3,4,8
field	paddock	4
filet	fillet	2
flashy dresser	galah	8
flies	blowies	4,5
flock	mob	4
food	tucker	2
football	gridiron	6
Fremantle, West Australia	Free-oh	7

Yank Term	Aussie Expression	Chapter
friend, pal, buddy	mate, digger, cobber	3
garbage collector	garbo	1
gasoline	petrol	5
gay man	camp man, poofter	3
gelatin	jelly	2
girl	Barossa pearl (RS)	3
go-cart	billycart	6
Good-bye!	Cheers! Hooroo!	4
granola	muesli	2
grapevine	bush telegraph	5
grocery store	milk bar	2
gum	chewie	2
guy	bloke	3
hard candy	boiled lollies	2
hat	tit-for-tat (RS)	1
hawker	spruiker	3
heating up	hotting up	4
hello	g'day	4
home remedy	bush cure	5
honest	fair dinkum, dinkum, dinky-di	2,4
Hong Kong	Honkers	7
hors d'oeuvres	savories	2
horseman	stockman, jackaroo	3
host, emcee	compere	3
housing development	housing estate	5
it will be okay	she'll be right.	4
itinerant, hobo	swagman; swaggie	4
jelly	jam	2
journalist	journo	1
jumpers	pinafores, pinnies	5

Yank Term	Aussie Expression	Chapter
ketchup or catsup	tomato sauce, sauce, dead horse (RS)	2
kids	billy lids (RS)	1
lawyer	solicitor, barrister	3
lay away	lay-by	5
leftovers	bubble and squeak	2
lefty	molly-dooker	6
lemon soda	lemonade	2
lifeguard competition	surf carnivals	6
lifeguards	surf lifesavers	6
line up	queue	5
linens	Manchester	5
liven it up	stir the possums	8
living room	lounge room	5
lobster	crayfish	2
lots (of things)	heaps	2
lucky	tinny	4
luncheonette	coffee lounge	2
M.V.P.	best and fairest	6
marking pen	Texta (brand)	5
Melbourne residents	Melburnians	7
messes things up	mucks it up	5
messy situation	a sticky wicket	6
Methodist	Metho	3
milkman	milko	1
mosquitoes	mozzies	4
motorcycle gang member	bikie	1
motorcycle rider	biker	1
Mrs. (wife)	cheese and kisses (RS)	1

Yank Term	Aussie Expression	Chapter
mushrooms	mushies	5
napkins	serviettes	5
New Zealander	Kiwi, Enzed	7
news anchor	presenter	3
No way!	Not on!	3
no rules at all	Rafferty's rules	4
nonsense	bizzo	4
nosey-body	steaky beak	4
not a chance	Buckley's chance	4
nothing to worry about	no worries	4
nude	bullocky, bols, starkers	4
outhouse	dunny	5
outlaw	bushranger	4
paddy wagon	divvy van	1
panties	knickers	5
parking lot	car park	1
pen, ballpoint	Biro (brand)	5
peppers	capsicum	5
pharmacist	chemist	3
phone	eau de cologne (RS); Al Capone (RS)	1
piano	goanna (RS)	8
politician	pollie	1
porch	veranda	5
position, place	possie	1
postman	postie	1
pot pie	meat pie	2
preacher	Bible-basher	3
Presbyterian	Presbo, Pressbutton	3
present, gift	prezzie	1
private schools	public schools	5

Yank Term	Aussie Expression	Chapter
public schools	state schools	5
pullover, sweater	jumper	5
Queensland	Banana Republic	7
Queenslander	Banana-bender	7
raft, inflatable	Lilo (brand)	6
ranch	station	4
red beets	beetroot	2
redneck	ocker	3
relatives	rellies, relos	1
rides like the wind	rides like Billyo	4
root (for a team)	barrack	4
rotten smelling	on the nose, gone off	2
row houses	terrace houses	5
ruffians, jerks	hoons, larrikans	3
sandwich	sanger, jaffle	2
sausages	bangers, snags	2
schoolbag	port, case	5
senior citizens	pensioners	6
shark	Noah's Ark (RS)	8
sheep	jumbuck	8
shorts	Stubbies (brand)	5
shrimp	prawn	3,8
sick, ill	crook	5
silly person	dilly (RS), Blinky Bill (RS)	3
Singapore	Singers	7
slot machines	pokies	6
snackbar	tuckshop	2
snakes	Joe Blakes (RS)	8
sneakers	sandshoes	5
soaking wet	wet as a shag	8
soap	Bob Hope (RS)	1

KANGAROO'S COMMENTS AND WALLABY'S WORDS

Yank Term	Aussie Expression	Chapter
soda	softdrinks	2
spongy cloth	Wettex (brand)	5
spouse, mate	china plate (RS)	1
squash	pumpkin	2
stag party, bachelor party	buck's party, buck's night	5
stained glass	leadlight	5
stand proud	sit up like Jacky	4
state fair (in Oz)	The Royal Show	4
stewardess	hostie	3
stupid person, an idiot (sarcastic)	bunny, drongo, raw prawn	3,8
suit	bag of fruit (RS)	1
supper	tea	2
surfers	surfies, boardies	6
sweatshirt	sloppy joe, windcheater	5
swimsuit	bathers, togs, cozzie, boardshorts	5,6
Sydney	Steak and Kidney (RS)	1,7
Sydney residents	Sydneysiders	7
takeout food	takeaway food	2
Tasmania	Tassie	7
tattletale	pimp	3
tease	take the mickey out	4
television	telly	1
terrific	beaut, bonzer, grouse, ripper	4
thrilled	happy as Larry, rapt, happy as a possum. . .	4,8

Glossary: American-Australian Reference

Yank Term	Aussie Expression	Chapter
to tattle	to pimp, to dingo	3,8
to gossip	split a bibful	4
to jerk (a car)	to kangaroo	8
toey	jumpy	4
toilet; bathroom	loo	5
track and field	athletics	6
turtleneck	polo collar jumper, skivvy	5
underarms	under the Warwicks (RS)	1
unsteady	dicky	4
vacation	holidays	1
Volkswagen	Veedub	5
wait a moment	just a tick	5
wander	go walkabout	4
waterhole	dam, bogie	4
week from Friday	Friday week	5
wife	trouble and strife (RS)	1
wild horse	brumby	8
wind funnel	willy-willy	4
within the sound of my voice	within coo-ee	4
woman	Sheila, bird	3
Woolworth's	Woolies	4
work	yakker	4
wrench	spanner	5
Z, the letter	zed	1

Bibliography

This bibliography offers additional titles for further reading on the meanings of Australian-English. The titles and the publishers are predominantly Australian and the books are available in Australian public libraries and bookstores. Some may be available in the United States in libraries or through specialty publishers.

Some of these titles were employed as reference material for this book, for checking spellings and etymologies, and making comparisons with the uses of phrases in everyday speech and how they've changed through the years.

My research into previously written material was completed mostly in the main library in Melbourne where some out-of-print books and university papers were also available; but because it is not material easily at hand in America or even during a casual visit to Australia, I have omitted those references here.

Baker, Sidney. *The Australian Language*, Second Edition. Sydney: Currawong Publishing Company, 1966.
———. *Australia Speaks*. Sydney: Shakespeare Head Press, 1953.

————. A *Dictionary of Australian Slang*, 1982 Edition. South Yarra, Victoria: O'Neil Publishers, 1959.

Hornadge, Bill. *The Australian Slanguage*. Sydney: Cassell Australia/Methuen Australia, 1980.

Macquarie University. *Aussie Talk*, "The Macquarie Dictionary of Australian Colloquialisms." McMahon's Point, N.S.W.: The Macquarie Library Pty. Ltd., 1984.

————. *The Macquarie Dictionary*. McMahon's Point, N.S.W.: The Macquarie Library Pty. Ltd., 1981.

O'Grady John. *Aussie English*. Sydney: Ambassador Press Pty. Ltd., 1965.

Partridge, Eric. *A Dictionary of Historical Slang*. Hammondsworth, England: Penguin Books Ltd., 1977.

————. *A Dictionary of Slang an Unconventional English*. Hammondsworth, England: Penguin Books Ltd., 1977.

Wilkes, G.A. *A Dictionary of Australian Colloquialisms*. Australia: Fontana Books/Australia, 1985.